A Leadership Guide for

SYNERGY

Church Staff and Volunteers

Ann A. Michel

Abingdon Press™
Nashville

SYNERGY:
A LEADERSHIP GUIDE FOR CHURCH STAFF AND VOLUNTEERS

Library of Congress Cataloging-in-Publication Data has been requested.

ISBN: 978-1-5018-3255-0

17 18 19 20 21 22 23 24 25 26—10 9 8 7 6 5 4 3 2 1

MANUFACTURED IN THE UNITED STATES OF AMERICA

Contents

Contents

Foreword

By Lovett H. Weems, Jr.

Myriad changes have reshaped the church in recent decades. Dr. Ann A. Michel explores one of those noteworthy changes that is widespread but rarely discussed. The proliferation of staffing beyond clergy, both within and outside congregations, has grown dramatically. These full-time and part-time positions are filled by committed lay people with many skills, though usually without formal theological training. Michel writes as someone who is lay, though she has two advanced theological degrees. She writes also from the perspective of one who has served many years as a lay professional on a church staff and, in more recent years, has made lay staffing a focus for extensive research and study. She describes the reasons for the growth of lay staff, but her primary focus is on providing valuable resources for lay staff who have a passion for ministry but not always the training and networks needed to flourish in their roles.

The challenges Michel addresses are shared among lay staff across church sizes and denominations. Issues such as theological identity, spiritual authority, and role ambiguity are common concerns. For the most part, while churches and denominational leaders appreciate the ministry of lay staff, few resources are available comparable to those clergy take for granted. Her positive message should give not only lay staff but also the clergy and others who work with them the tools they need to begin helping these invaluable ministers flourish even more than they are now.

Lay staff need the abundant biblical and theological grounding they will find in this book. They will be enriched by it and draw courage and inspiration as they see how deeply woven their form of ministry is with the entire history of the Christian church. Another part of the book helps lay staff with skills they need for the daily work they do. Discovering help for securing volunteers, building teams, addressing conflict, developing others, and managing meetings will enhance ministry for all, including those in ministry for many years.

But there is a bigger story being told here. While lay staff will appreciate their theological validation and enrichment for work skills, perhaps the most important message is that the author understands the expansion of ministry opportunities for laity as a key component of the revitalization of the Christian church. Instead of seeing the growth of lay staff as a necessary result of less money in churches or fewer clergy, she sees this movement as a working of God's Spirit in a new way in our time. This is one of the reasons that *Synergy* is an appropriate title. God is taking this more diverse and inclusive model of how churches function and using it for things greater than the sum of individual activities. Clergy and laity no longer need to tussle for more power, because they now discover that out of the synergistic power of God, one plus one can actually equal more than two. There is no end to what God can do when all are committed to the guiding purpose and when a diversity of gifts and perspectives are richly available to fulfill the purpose.

Remember that Paul describes the church as the "body" of Christ, not a collection of body parts. The synergy needed must go beyond clergy and lay staff to include the entire people of God. Laity who are staff have their own ministries, and much of the work of both clergy and lay staff is to liberate the passion that all laity have to embody their faith through service and spiritual growth. The synergy is not complete unless the gifts of all are manifest in the witness of the congregation.

One of the great strengths of this book is the authenticity of the author as someone who models that about which she writes. In numerous roles and settings, she exemplifies the power of working together to accomplish far more than the collection of individual tasks. Never forget that laity in ministry, as well as clergy, are there to reflect God's love, model Christ's example of servanthood, and renew God's vision for the church and the world.

Introduction

I n recent decades, the practice of ministry became more diverse, varied, and inclusive in several significant ways. One of the most notable changes is the increasing number of lay persons who take on significant ministry roles. In our churches today, tens of thousands of lay staff workers provide Christian nurture to our children, counsel our youth, and lead ministries that engage others in Christian formation, education, and outreach. They conduct worship, and they support and order the life of the church in myriad vital ways.

A few years ago, I undertook extensive research to document the extent and nature of the growth of lay staff ministry in my own denomination, The United Methodist Church. By using quantitative and qualitative research strategies, I estimated that 40,000 lay staff (full-time and part-time) work in United Methodist congregations. Apparently, more lay persons than ordained elders receive church paychecks.[1] Similar trends exist in other denominations and in nondenominational congregations as well. The US Catholic Church, for example, has more than 30,000 lay persons in its ecclesial workforce, and since the 1990s, the number of lay workers has surpassed the number of priests in parish ministry.[2]

Many other lay ministry practitioners work in settings beyond the local church—on the mission field, in ministries of community service, in parachurch organizations, in denominational agencies and programs, and in theological education. They serve as certified lay ministers, deaconesses, and lay missioners. And hundreds of thousands of lay persons have serious commitments to unpaid or volunteer ministries.

A new and different approach to ministry is also emerging among younger leaders who know that the green, growing edges of the Christian faith are often found beyond the institutional confines of traditional church settings. For many years, a growing percentage of seminary graduates opt against ordination and service in traditional congregational settings. They feel led to go where they perceive that the Spirit is most active—within their communities and in places where faith intersects daily life. If you are reading this book, it's likely that you are already part of this ministry trend.

While my particular interest is lay ministry, the trend toward a more diverse and inclusive paradigm of ministry is evident within ordained ministry and the pastorate as well. There are more women clergy. Several denominations have restored the permanent diaconate. And an increasing percentage of churches are served by pastors in various forms of licensed and certified ministry.

Synergy addresses this changing landscape of ministry to support a more inclusive, collaborative paradigm of ministry that affirms the gifts and callings of these new church leaders. This book can serve as a training manual for lay church workers to help them understand how their ministry relates to the mission of God and the ministry of the church and to provide practical guidance on interpersonal ministry skills essential to any expression of collaborative ministry.

REASONS FOR THE GROWTH IN LAY STAFFING

The growth in lay staff ministry is fueled by several factors. The lay empowerment movement, the growth of multi-staff megachurches, a changing culture of volunteerism, and the demand for specialized programmatic ministries are part of the trend. And some clergy prepared primarily to be preachers and caregivers don't have the skills or the inclination to develop and manage programmatic ministries, work primarily with children or youth, or give major emphasis to administrative matters. So as expressions of church become more diverse and expansive, laity are standing in the gap. And church members increasingly look to lay staff for the type of leadership, counsel, instruction, and spiritual direction once provided exclusively by clergy.

There are dollar-and-cents factors at work as well. Lay staff generally cost less than clergy, who can come with minimum salary and benefits requirements as well as housing allowances. And congregations generally can exercise more control in the hiring and termination of lay staff. In smaller congregations, particularly those that can't support full-time clergy, paid and unpaid lay persons are assuming many vital ministry functions.

CHALLENGES FACED BY LAY MINISTRY PRACTITIONERS

The growth in lay staffing is scarcely news to anyone involved in the day-to-day work of churches, for these trends have persisted for several decades. Yet our mind-set about ministry isn't quick to change. The institutional structures that support ministry—

denominational agencies, connectional structures, and theological education—are slow to adapt to this evolving landscape. For this reason and others, lay ministry practitioners are often ill-prepared and underappreciated, confused about their call, and unsure of their theological identity. I offer *Synergy* in response to this reality—to help clergy, laity, and congregations embrace this more inclusive paradigm of ministry.

Lay servants face three distinct but interrelated challenges. First, lay ministry practitioners experience role ambiguities and tensions, particularly related to their theological identity and spiritual authority. While the theology of pastoral identity is well established, the identity of lay persons in ministry is often less clearly understood. We are in many ways betwixt and between. Some congregants look to lay staff as spiritual leaders while others lack respect for our spiritual authority. We are often expected to assume the attitudes, protocols, and responsibilities associated with ordained ministry while at the same time bumping up against the expectation that ministry is the work of the ordained.

For example, people often ask me why I've never entered the ministry. They can't understand why someone with two advanced theological degrees and more than twenty years of full-time Christian service doesn't bear the title Reverend, doesn't wear a robe or a stole, and generally sits in the pews on Sunday mornings. "I am in ministry" is my unwavering response. But somehow, this answer doesn't always sit right with people. Some express annoyance that I won't claim the title they think my education has earned. Some clergy friends are honest enough to confess they are unnerved by a lay person capable of teaching and leading them. And I know that colleagues take people aside before introducing me to explain my credentials lest someone assume that I'm "just" a lay person. Don't get me wrong. I've been blessed with amazing opportunities to lead and learn and teach and serve. But it seems that even in an era when we talk constantly about lay empowerment, people are more than a little surprised when they encounter a fully empowered lay person. At some level, it disrupts deeply rooted assumptions about what ministry is and who is a minister. Given the growing number of laity seriously engaged in ministry today, there is a need to articulate a more robust and compelling theology of lay ministry.

Second, many lay ministry practitioners come into church work with backgrounds in other professions and generally lack formal theological training. They may be gifted musicians, teachers, counselors, or administrators, but they do not necessarily know the nuances of church leadership. And they have few resources that address their particular situation. Seminary curricula generally assume the paradigm of ordained ministry and regard the work of solo pastors as normative. Most church leadership books are written by clergy for clergy, usually from the vantage point of a senior or solo pastor. Even books that address newer patterns of ministry are generally written *about* lay engagement rather than being written *to* and *for* an audience of laity. In short, lay ministry practitioners need leadership advice that addresses their challenges and needs.

Finally, lay persons who are church employees tend to function in an ill-defined gray area regarding their professional status and responsibilities. This is particularly true for the growing number of church employees who are also members of the church they serve. Denominations tend to have clear structures and policies regarding clergy supervision, accountability, support, and growth. But similar structures for lay persons in professional ministry are often lacking. Lay ministry often occurs beneath the radar screen of institutions beyond the local church, including judicatories, denominational agencies, and theological seminaries, so there are very few resources or guidelines addressing the unique situation of lay staff.

Synergy is written in response to these three challenges. The first part of this book presents a theological framework to undergird a more inclusive, collaborative understanding of ministry that affirms the gifts and calling of both clergy and lay servants. The book's first three chapters explore synergistic ministry as a theological narrative that supports and affirms this growing diversity and fullness of ministry.

The second part of the book is more practical in focus. Chapters 4 through 9 equip lay servants with the day-to-day skills of collaborative ministry: how to nurture relationships, how to build teams, how to engage others in ministry, how to develop others as leaders, how to manage meetings, and how to deal with conflicts and complaints. This shift from theology to practice may seem like a transition from the sublime to the ridiculous, as the focus in these chapters is often quite tactical. However, the tactics are only effective when grounded in faith, gratitude, and an appreciation for the relational dimension of incarnational ministry. Synergy is a matter of both belief and practice, and the two can't be separated.

The final part of the book addresses issues commonly faced by church employees but seldom addressed in the church workplace, such as how the role of a staff member differs from the role of a church member, finding space for personal spiritual growth, and matters of confidentiality and boundaries. It also considers how church employees can grow in effectiveness and in spiritual maturity by taking responsibility for their own professional development. The issues and recommendations flow from the findings of my research with lay ministry professionals.

A PERSONAL PERSPECTIVE

Synergy draws together my long-standing interest in the theology and practice of lay ministry and the knowledge of leadership effectiveness I have gained serving for the past twelve years at the Lewis Center for Church Leadership of Wesley Theological Seminary. The book also draws on my experience as a lay ministry practitioner at Metropolitan Memorial United Methodist Church in Washington, DC, where I served in several different staff roles over the better part of a decade before joining the Lewis Center staff. While I lift up a number of examples from my own experience, I feel compelled to acknowledge that my personal leadership hasn't always measured up to the standards of this book. In many ways, I have written *Synergy* to be the spiritual and practical resource I needed but didn't have when I started down this path.

Also, my thinking about the respective roles of clergy and laity has evolved over the course of this journey. I first came into church leadership in the heyday of the lay empowerment movement of the 1990s. It was tempting to blame all the church's problems on clericalism. Eschewing ordination to pursue lay ministry, I inwardly regarded myself as a conscientious objector within a system that elevated clergy and denigrated laity. But now I think of myself as a conscientious affirmer. I believe that the church desperately needs deeply committed, theologically astute, and effective lay leaders, and I attempt to model that in my own work. I believe equally that the church desperately needs deeply committed, theologically astute, and effective clergy leaders. I see nothing to be gained in clergy and laity blaming each other for the church's ills. In *Synergy*, I present a more inclusive, collaborative way of thinking about ministry that affirms the work of both clergy and lay servants, transcending the old dividing-line paradigm of ministry that places clergy and laity in contradistinction to each other.

Clergy as well as laity benefit from a more inclusive, synergistic paradigm of ministry. When holiness and Christ-like living are seen as the special purview of the clergy, they labor under unrealistic expectations that can lead to stress, isolation, and burnout. Moreover, when ordained ministry is seen as the only "real" ministry and the only way of acting on or legitimizing one's call, then everyone interested in serving God feels the need to be ordained. This encourages those with marginal gifts for the ministries of Word, sacrament, and order to seek ordination. This, I believe, is one reason there are so many issues today around questions of clergy effectiveness. When all types of ministry are honored and affirmed, people are free to serve in the area of their particular giftedness.

Some people regard the proliferation of ministry roles and the expansion of lay ministry as a regrettable consequence of congregations in decline, a challenge to the distinctive status of ordained ministry, and a diminution of the authority of clergy. But I believe it's an act of the Spirit to renew the church. In a time when the church is groaning under the tremendous stresses and strains of institutional decline, I believe that God is raising up the leaders needed to serve God's mission in this day and inviting us to reclaim the synergistic approach to leadership that God intended from the start. It's in this spirit that I offer *Synergy* as a resource to the church, with hopes that it will help both ordained and lay servants bend the shape of their ministries to follow the Spirit's leading.

PART ONE

SYNERGISTIC
MINISTRY

Working Together

God's Plan for the Church

T he English word *synergy* comes from the Greek word *synergos*, which means "working together." In English usage, however, the term implies something more than merely working together. In a synergistic relationship, the whole represents more than the sum of its parts. Synergistic relationships are dynamic, and their impact is exponential. The positive, collaborative force of synergistic relationships gives rise to added energy and efficacy. Synergistic phenomena occur in the natural world, in the realm of behavioral science, and in economic relationships.

You've probably experienced synergy when working as part of a well-functioning team. Everyone is fully engaged and appreciates the importance of the work. Individuals understand their unique role and how their contribution is essential to the group's mission. There is positive energy. Things just seem to click and flow because of the nature of the group dynamic.

Synergy is a powerful force because it's part of God's plan. Indeed, synergy is part of the very essence of our triune God. Divine power and energy emanate from the relational character of God, from the interplay between Father, Son, and Spirit. The three Persons of the Trinity are distinct and different yet equal and mutually affirming.

Our synergistic God wants and expects us to work together synergistically. We see this clearly in the ministry of Jesus. One of his first acts of public ministry was to form a team. He placed a tremendous priority on nurturing his community of disciples and developing other leaders, which made possible the exponential growth of the early Christian movement following his death and resurrection.[1] "Had the church relied on a single, incredibly gifted, magnetic individual to replace Jesus, the church would surely have collapsed."[2]

We see it also in the biblical record of Paul's mission. The book of Acts and the Pauline Epistles name more than one hundred individuals who were Paul's partners in ministry. Paul even refers to some of these co-workers using the Greek term *synergos*.[3] We tend to regard Jesus and Paul as individual actors and solitary leaders because we read Scripture through lenses tainted by our cultural preoccupation with individualism. But as New Testament scholar Efrain Agosto observes, "Both Jesus and Paul refused to work alone."[4] They understood the power and necessity of a synergistic approach to ministry.

GOD'S BLUEPRINT FOR SYNERGISTIC TEAMWORK

In 1 Corinthians, Paul speaks of the church as the body of Christ composed of a variety of interdependent, indispensable parts (1 Cor 12:12-18). By using the metaphor of a human body, he reminds us that our feet and our hands, our eyes and our ears are all equally part of our bodies. "If the whole body were an eye, what would happen to the hearing? And if the whole body were an ear, what would happen to the sense of smell? . . . So the eye can't say to the hand, 'I don't need you,' or in turn, the head can't say to the feet, 'I don't need you'"(1 Cor 12:17, 21 CEB). And Paul reminds us that even those body parts we think of as less respectable are essential to our health and worthy of great honor. The human body can only function properly when each of our organs does what it was designed to do.

This teaching illuminates how we in the church are to work together. The metaphor reveals that synergy is enhanced when there is unity in diversity and mutual respect. It tells us that no part or member of the body of Christ is less essential than any other. It allows for the distinctness of various ministries while reinforcing the need for collaboration and mutuality. And it reminds us that truly synergistic ministry is humble and subservient rather than hierarchical, since Christ, not any particular category of ecclesial servants, heads the Body (Col 1:18). We are to work together in harmony under the headship of Christ.

While Paul's allusion to the human body is metaphorical, this teaching is neither fanciful nor trivial. It's God's blueprint for how Christian servants—lay and ordained, paid and unpaid—are expected to be in ministry together. It's a biblical mandate for ministry as synergistic teamwork. It's a template for how we are to serve together and respect each other in a day when expressions of ministry are becoming more multifaceted and diverse.

Too often, though, we approach the work of the church in ways that don't fully embody this synergistic potential. We cling to an outdated mental model of ministry that assumes one pivotal leader and many followers, generally an ordained clergyperson laboring alone as the sole pastor attending to the spiritual needs of a particular flock. This way of thinking about ministry is deeply ingrained in our institutional structures and our cultural imagination. It's embedded also in how we prepare people for ministry and teach the disciplines of church leadership. As a result, our clergy leaders often feel overburdened and burned out. And those of us among the growing cadre of lay servants find ourselves confused about our theological identity, our spiritual authority, and how we can lead in the church. This tendency to think too narrowly about ministry limits the practice of ministry at a time when the service of God requires more ministry—not less. It divides clergy and laity at a time when greater collaboration is needed.

RECLAIMING THE SYNERGISTIC APPROACH

The church today faces tremendous challenges, and change is unlikely to come if we remain locked in an outdated mind-set about ministry. God is inviting us to enlarge our understandings of leadership and reimagine how the work of the church will be carried forward. God is inviting us to step away from culturally defined notions of ministry that equate it with position and profession, power and privilege, and to step back into God's plan for how the mission of God is to be carried forward. God is inviting us to embrace a more inclusive, collaborative approach to ministry that more fully engages lay servants, both paid and unpaid. I believe this is why the Spirit of God is calling so many lay persons to various types of ministry in this day.

- Synergistic ministry is a theological narrative that supports and affirms the growing diversity and fullness of ministry.

- Synergistic ministry understands that all ministry

originates with God. It isn't the possession, privilege, or prerogative of any human agent or institution.

- Synergistic ministry is an extension of the servanthood of Jesus, not a matter of position, power, or professional standing.

- Synergistic ministry is limitless because when ministry is properly defined as service, there can never be too much ministry or too many ministers.

- Synergistic ministry is predicated on the whole people of God being called to serve God and one another.

- Synergistic ministry is inherently relational and collaborative. It never rests on the accomplishments of a solitary individual and can't be reduced to a single office.

CLAIMING OUR SPIRITUAL BIRTHRIGHT

When our practice of ministry is grounded in these beliefs, we unlock the spiritual potential that was present at the start of the church. On the day of Pentecost, the Spirit birthed the church in a burst of synergistic energy. On that day, the disciples were all gathered in one place. The Spirit filled the whole room and rested on each individual. Not on a single individual but on each of the disciples. Not just the twelve but all 120 who were gathered in that room (Acts 1:15). The gift they were given, of being able to speak in other languages, equipped them to reach and engage even more people. This energy bore tremendous fruit as day by day the Lord added to their number (Acts 2).

Peter understood that this was a fulfillment of Joel's prophecy that God would pour God's Spirit out on all flesh—men and women, old and young, slave and free (Acts 2:17-18). In the Old

Testament era, spiritual immediacy and authority rested with a few remarkable figures, such as prophets or religious authorities.[5] But with the coming of the Spirit, meaningful leadership is no longer limited to the usual suspects. "This promise is for you, your children, and for all who are far away," said Peter, "as many as the Lord our God invites" (Acts 2:39 CEB).

This synergistic energy propelled the growth of the early church as many different expressions of ministry arose spontaneously, each grounded in a charism, or gift, of the Spirit. The sheer number of individuals named in the New Testament and the variety of tasks and services ascribed to them indicate the breadth and inclusivity of the ministry in the primitive church. There were apostles, prophets, teachers, and leaders, as well as healers, helpers, and miracle workers (1 Cor 12:28-29). Others served as evangelists and pastors (Eph 4:11) and as hosts or heads of house churches. There were bishops, deacons, and elders,[6] although the use of these terms in the New Testament doesn't necessarily correspond to the way these offices evolved in the later history of the church.

As the church matured over centuries, ministry became more institutionalized and ordered. But could it be that the Spirit is inviting us to reclaim the synergy that is part of our spiritual heritage? To think of ministry not as a calling for the few but for the many? We know that God continues to pour God's Spirit out on all flesh. On you. On me. On clergy and laity alike. On everyone whom God calls. And the Spirit continues to gift each of us for ministry. God is empowering, equipping, and calling us to serve. While recognizing this great gift, let us embrace the synergy that is at the heart of God and God's will for the people of God.

Discussion Questions

1. When have you experienced synergy? What contributed to the experience of synergy?

2. Why do you think that synergy is part of God's plan for the church? Based on what you've read so far, what do you think are key elements of synergy in the church?

3. Can you think of factors that impede synergy in your congregation or ministry setting?

CHAPTER TWO
Who, Me? Yes, You!

The Inclusivity of God's Call

What comes to mind when you imagine God calling people into ministry? A thunderous voice from a mountaintop? A burning bush? Angelic messengers? An audible voice calling in the night? A palpable, metaphysical tap on the shoulder? Scripture and other testimony give witness to how God sometimes reaches out to people in these dramatic ways. But God calls people in more subtle and ordinary ways as well.

As a seminary student, I discovered that classmates who were candidates for ordination were often asked to share their call stories. They were encouraged to spend considerable time discerning and describing their call. As they presented their call narratives to others, they became more refined and rehearsed, and their sense of call solidified. But because I was not preparing for ordination, not a single person in my congregation or my seminary ever asked me to think about whether my desire to serve God was a call.

Over the centuries, our understanding of call became distorted by the notion that it's reserved for certain categories of "holy people"—priests, monks, nuns, and clergy. And there can be such a mystique surrounding whom God calls and how God calls them that lay persons are left feeling spiritually deficient. We wonder whether God could possibly be calling us as well.

GOD CALLS EVERYONE

Part of the great good news is that call isn't reserved for a select group of spiritual elites or ecclesiastical offices. God is calling each and every one of us to faith and to a particular role in the body of Christ. Since ministry is correctly defined as service and all Christians are called to follow Christ's example of servanthood, it follows that all Christians are called to ministry. The New Testament word most used for the whole community of Christ-followers is *ecclesia*, which means those "called out." To be a Christian, to be part of the church, is to be called, chosen, and set aside for service to God.[1]

Protestant theology tends to distinguish between two types of call—a primary or general call to the life of faith and a secondary or particular call to a specific task or role.[2] The problem comes when the idea of a particular calling is understood to apply only to those called to ordained ministry. In his wonderful book *The Call*, Os Guinness illustrates this problem by drawing on the story of William Wilberforce, the eighteenth-century British abolitionist who led the fifty-year struggle to end the English slave trade. In 1785, at the age of twenty-five, Wilberforce experienced a profound evangelical conversion. Like many others before and since, he thought that the only appropriate way to respond to his sense of calling was to leave politics and take up the life of a cleric in the Church of England. Fortunately, John Newton, the converted slave trader who wrote "Amazing Grace," persuaded him otherwise. After much prayer and discernment, Wilberforce concluded that God was calling him to champion the cause of the oppressed through his service in the political arena. Because Wilberforce had been captive to the erroneous belief that God's call is reserved for clergy, he came within a hair's breadth of missing his true calling—a calling that changed the lives of countless individuals and bent the course of world history toward greater alignment with God's justice.[3]

Survey responses from lay staff workers constitute a staggering testimony of the unique ministry of those called to serve on the front lines of local church ministry. A church bookkeeper sees herself as a steward assuring that church funds are spent wisely. Another office worker took the opportunity to minister every payday by writing encouragements from Scripture on the church employees' paystubs. A preschool director sees her role as an opportunity to reach unchurched families, to foster positive relationships that might lead them to Christ, and to be a spiritual leader for the preschool staff. A church musician told me, "I have the opportunity to do more than 'perform' but to give glory to God through the arts, the opportunity to participate in some small capacity in God changing someone's life through something I've done, and possibly the opportunity for someone to come to know Christ through the art I've helped present." As I read and analyzed their survey responses, I sensed I was reading a collective call narrative testifying to the inclusivity of God's call to ministry. Indeed, approximately 90 percent of the church employees I surveyed understood their work to be a calling, yet many had to figure it out for themselves without encouragement from others in the church.

God's call is open and inclusive because the spiritual gifts needed to carry forth God's mission are widely dispersed among us all. Remember God's blueprint for synergistic ministry in 1 Corinthians 12? Paul says that each of us is given a manifestation of the Spirit for the common good. Some receive the gift of wisdom, some the gift of knowledge; others receive the gift of faith, or healing, and so on (1 Cor 12:7-11). Because the gifts of the Spirit are bestowed widely and generously among all of us, God's call must be equally broad to activate each of us whose service is essential to God's mission. On a practical and personal level, this means that God is likely calling you in your areas of giftedness. Ask yourself and ask others, "What am I really good at?" This simple question can provide important clues regarding how God has gifted you and to what type of service God is calling you.

DISCERNING GOD'S CALL

God is capable of calling people in an infinite variety of ways. We live in an era when most people are not called with a trumpet blast from heaven. Each of us listens for "whispers of call" in the events of our lives and the quiet of our hearts.[4] Your calling may be discerned in a combination of what you feel passionate about, what you are capable of doing, and what others ask you to do. Sometimes, God's call becomes clear to us when we feel a compelling sense of purpose and drive that pushes us in a particular direction. For me, it became clear when I couldn't imagine any path forward in my life except a life of Christian service.

Sometimes, we see more clearly in retrospect the way God is calling and leading us. It can be helpful to reflect back on the path your life has taken. What clues are in the events and circumstances of your spiritual journey and life story? What were significant turning points? What people and events influenced you?

And sometimes, other people see in us what we are not able to see clearly in ourselves. Friends, family members, fellow church members, colleagues, or partners in ministry can open our eyes to signs of God's calling on our lives. Because call is never a private matter, the faith community plays an essential role in naming and affirming our gifts and helping discern our call to particular ministries.

ONE CALL

Unfortunately, well-intended Christians sometimes misinterpret the meaning of their call. I've known leaders who refuse to deviate from their own personal agenda, saying, "I have to be faithful to my call." And sadly, I've known leaders who use their call as a bully club to deflect criticism or pull rank on fellow church members. But our call from God isn't a personal possession or something that gives us special power or privilege. It's not a spiritual entitlement that obliges others to defer to our authority. It's a gift from God. It's a sacred responsibility to be lived out not for ourselves but for others.

Sometimes we imagine that some people receive a calling of a different order or magnitude. For example, we assume the call to ordained ministry is a higher calling. And sometimes we think that people who experience God's call in dramatic or direct ways are somehow "more called" or called to more worthy ministries. But in Christ's body, no member is more or less essential than any other member, so each of our callings is equally important. There can be no hierarchy within God's call. If some people experience God's call more intensely or urgently, I sometimes jokingly suggest that it may just mean that God had to work harder to get their attention! Just as there is one body and one Spirit, one faith, one hope, and one baptism (Eph 4:4-16), there is also but one call. All are called. And all callings are equally important.

THE SYNERGY OF CALL

Synergy is enhanced when each of us plays the role for which God has uniquely gifted us. God's call is an instrument of synergy because it guides us to our most meaningful and effective place of service—where our unique contribution magnifies the impact of others. God's call is energizing because it imbues our lives with a special sense of direction and dynamism that propels synergistic ministry.

Imagine the synergistic potential of a church where not just the clergy but every staff member, every leader, and every member understood themselves to be uniquely gifted and called to a particular ministry! All we have to do is listen and respond to unleash this energy. "Who, me?" you may ask. "Yes, YOU!" God is calling even you.

Discussion Questions

1. What comes to mind when you think of someone being called by God?

2. Do you understand yourself to be called to the work you do? If so, how would you describe that call? How did it come about? How has God confirmed it?

3. In what ways have others supported or inhibited your sense of call?

4. Trace your journey into church leadership. What were the significant turning points? What people and events influenced you? Where, in retrospect, do you see that God was leading or calling you?

5. Have you seen God expand or redirect your call to ministry over time? If so, in what ways has it changed? Where do you see God taking you in ministry in the years to come?

6. Draft a brief narrative of your call that you could share with others.

CHAPTER THREE
At Your Service

Ministry Grounded In God's Purposes

While setting aside what you know about the true nature of ministry, think for a minute about what the average pew-sitter in your church or the average person on the street thinks about ministry. They may be most familiar with the ceremonial roles performed by clergy, such as officiating at weddings or funerals or leading worship. Unless disaffected from the church, they may see ministry as an esteemed profession and think clergy are holier or closer to God than others. And they likely assume that the primary focus of ministry involves the internal, institutional life of the church. It can be hard for them to imagine that someone who doesn't conform to these expectations could be a minister.

Many of these ideas about ministry have their roots in medieval Catholicism when priests came to be understood as essential mediators between God and humankind. By virtue of their sacramental authority, they enjoyed a mystical, exalted aura that placed them nearer to God than ordinary Christians. For the laity, the Christian faith became more spiritualized and less active. Lay persons participated in the life of the church symbolically through ritual and sacrament.[1] It was a dualistic world in which clergy and laity were defined in contradistinction to each other. Clergy were ministers; laity were objects of ministry. Clergy were the spiritual elites; laity were passive spiritual consumers. Clergy concerned themselves with the sacred realm and the institutional life of the church; lay persons were concerned with the temporal or secular realm.

The Protestant Reformation challenged many of these assumptions. But certain elements of this dualistic paradigm of ministry are still very deeply entwined in the church's institutional identity. Despite reforms and doctrinal changes, they linger today, both in the church and in the collective consciousness of our culture, impeding the synergy possible in more collaborative approaches to ministry.

MINISTRY AS SERVICE

In Scripture we find a more inclusive understanding of ministry. The generic New Testament term for ministry is the Greek word *diakonia*, which denotes the humble service of a slave.[2] The Greek terms for servant and service appear over and over again in the New Testament—more than one hundred times and throughout all the books and letters.[3] Paul used this term consistently to refer to his own apostolic ministry and the work of other leaders in the community.[4] Our English word *ministry* has its origin in the Greek work *diakonia* (in Latin, *ministerium*), which is best translated simply as *service*.[5] "The word *service* was selected because the early Christians remembered how Jesus himself had come to serve and not be served," writes Kenan Osborne in the book *Orders and Ministry*. He says, "Service leadership, therefore, has been and remains the most basic foundation for all ministries in the Christian church."[6]

To affirm that ministry is service is to understand ministry as an action verb. It involves doing something for the sake of the gospel in the world. Ministry isn't an office or a designation. It isn't a state of mind, an order of being, or an ontological classification. It's something that we do. Every Christian is called to ministry because we are all commanded to serve each other in love.

Christians and non-Christians engage in service to their neighbors and their communities. However, the Christian's act of service becomes ministry when it's a visible sign of God's love in the world. A task becomes a ministry when it is undertaken as a way of participating in God's mission. For this reason, motivation is critical to ministry. The credibility and authority of any ministry is ultimately found in the extent to which it reflects God's purposes. Ministry exists to serve God's mission of redeeming and transforming the world. In every arena where we work, God is already at work. We are invited to be partners in God's mission, yet it originates with God. Therefore, ministry isn't the possession, privilege, or prerogative of any human agent or institution, because ministry belongs to God.

WE'RE IN THIS TOGETHER

Historically, definitions of ministry identify the characteristics that distinguish one class of believers and servants from another. So, for example, in my denomination, different orders of ordained ministry and different types of pastoral leaders are distinguished by such things as who is allowed to perform the sacraments and other rites of the church in different ministry settings. There are even rules about who is allowed to wear the stole, a symbol of servanthood that evokes the memory of Christ's service in washing his disciples' feet. But synergistic ministry demands that we think less about what distinguishes different ministries and instead about what all expressions of ministry have in common—what some contemporary theologians describe as a "common matrix" of ministry.[7] A common matrix defines ministry as grounded in relationships of service and trust, inaugurated in baptism, and vested in the whole people of God.

In the opening chapters of each of the four Gospels, we learn Jesus's public ministry and his life in the Spirit were inaugurated with his baptism. So too for us, it's the laying on of hands in baptism, not the laying on of hands in ordination, that authorizes a life of ministry. "The distinctiveness of this or that ministry is properly understood only in the light of the common foundation of all ministries in baptism. All ministers, ordained and nonordained, are first and finally members of God's Holy People, who are consecrated for mission."[8] Through baptism, every Christian in the church is authorized and empowered for mission within the church and in the world.

Some have referred to Jesus and his followers as a lay renewal movement because they posed an alternative to the established patterns of religious leadership in first-century Judaism, including the hereditary priesthood.[9] Not surprisingly, given Jesus's frequent criticism of the religious authorities of his day, the New Testament community rejected *priest* as a term for its leaders. In the New Testament, the term *priest* is used only to refer to the whole people of God, or to Christ himself as high priest (Heb 7:24-26). In 1 Peter, we read, "You yourselves are being built like living stones into a spiritual temple. You are being made into a holy priesthood" (1 Pet 2:5 CEB) and "you are a chosen race, a royal priesthood, a holy nation, a people who are God's own possession" (1 Pet 2:9 CEB). The book of Revelation describes how God's saints from every tribe, language, people, and nation have been made to be priests serving God (Rev 5:9-10). In these passages, the priesthood is a function of the whole church rather than certain individuals.[10] This doctrine of the priesthood of all believers, revived by Martin Luther during the Reformation, is another cornerstone in a common matrix of ministry.

THE LANGUAGE OF SYNERGY

In the passage above, the writer of 1 Peter uses the term *laos*—the source of our words *lay* and *laity*—to describe the church as the people of God. And yet, in common parlance, these terms have come to mean inexpert, amateur, inexperienced, or ordinary. Even within the church, there is a tendency to think of laity as secondary, as a lesser order of Christians. Because synergy rests on the power of the whole people of God in ministry together, we need to guard against the denigration of these terms. Those of us who are lay servants can embrace the biblical definition of laity as "the people of God" and affirm that clergy and laity are both equally a part of God's people.

When it comes to matters of inclusiveness, words matter. And there are other ways the language of ministry subtly—and sometimes not so subtly—impedes synergy. For example, one of our dominant metaphors for ministry posits clergy as shepherds or pastors and the congregation as a flock of sheep, which isn't exactly the most challenging or enlightened image of Christian personhood and discipleship. And yet this is the way we talk about God's people—as a flock of helpless animals. Synergy requires a new, more inclusive, empowering language of faith and ministry—one that affirms the gifts and calling of laity and clergy alike. Paul's image of the church as the body of Christ is a more egalitarian metaphor for the church than the imagery of shepherd and flock.

When we reduce ministry to power, position, or institutional prerogative, it becomes a zero-sum game. It must be controlled tightly and doled out sparingly. Much energy is wasted debating matters of authority and privilege. Dividing ministry into smaller and smaller pieces restricts synergy. It limits the practice of ministry at a time when the service of God and the needs of God's world require more ministry, not less. When ministry is properly viewed as service undertaken on behalf of God's purposes, ministry becomes infinite. There can never be too much ministry or too many ministers. A broad and diverse ministry is a natural outgrowth of the mission of the gospel in the face of the multiplicity of human needs and the diverse circumstances to which the church is called to minister. It's a manifestation of the synergistic energy of God.

Discussion Questions

1. What images come first to your mind when you think of ministry?

2. Reflect on what it means to understand ministry as service.

3. Name some people you think are ministers, given this definition of ministry. What is notable about them?

4. Spend some time unpacking the various meanings of the terms *lay* and *laity* in the church and in our culture. How can we reclaim the biblical meaning of laity as the people of God?

PART TWO

Collaborative Ministry Skills for Synergistic Leaders

CHAPTER FOUR

The Heart of the Matter

The Power of Relationships

T he power of relationships is at the heart of synergistic ministry. Theologically, the inherently relational character of ministry is another aspect of the common matrix that defines
ministry. The ultimate identity and purpose of each member of
Christ's body is derived not from our individual status or specific
tasks but in our relationships of service.[1] Whether ministry is clas-
sified as lay or ordained, whether it's paid or unpaid, all ministry is
rooted in the relational life and mission of the triune God.

Just as the theology of shared ministry is grounded in a common foundation of relationships, so too is the practice of shared
ministry. Lovett H. Weems, Jr., observes that "relationships are
everything. Just as all Christian leadership originates in our relationship with Christ, our day-by-day leadership depends on relationships with others that mirror the ideals of our faith. . . . A
relational foundation is essential for leaders."[2]

Synergistic leaders gain their influence and effectiveness by
building and maintaining a network of relationships. Whether
you are a Christian educator, an administrator, a musician, or a
worship leader, your ability to do what God is calling you to do
ultimately depends on how well you relate to others. If you are

naturally extroverted, the relational dimension of ministry may come easily to you. Introverts might need to be a bit more intentional. But all church leaders need to develop habits and practices that create synergy by reinforcing the bonds of love and trust within Christ's body.

WHY RELATIONSHIPS MATTER

For years, I've been involved through my church in a community organizing network in the city I call home, the District of Columbia. All the participants in this extensive grassroots movement are committed to a shared discipline where each of us regularly seeks out opportunities to sit down and have one-on-one conversations with others—often people we don't know, people who might be different from us in any number of ways. We are trained to get beyond superficial pleasantries and standard chit-chat and ask more probing questions. What makes you tick? What do you value? What angers you? What motivates you to act?

This conversational discipline is critical to community organizing because power is relational. In the context of these relationships we discover mutual interests that inspire us to work together in common purpose. We expand our networks of influence. We learn to see past our differences and trust one another. I've witnessed the transformative power of these relationships over twenty years, as people of faith from different parts of our city have transcended the barriers of religion, race, and socioeconomic status to stand together for the common good.

The power of relationships fuels synergy in other expressions of ministry as well. As we invest in developing meaningful relationships with other people, they come to know and trust us, to respect our motives, and to feel affinity with our objectives. They are more willing to give us the benefit of the doubt, support us when we take risks, and have our back when the going gets tough. The trust and credibility born of interpersonal encounter are the relational capital that allows leaders to lead.

At the most fundamental level, as our relational networks expand, we know more people with whom we can engage in shared ministry. Recruiting is a constant challenge for most ministry leaders. And the best recruiters are generally those who have lots of friends and acquaintances whom they can tap. People are naturally inclined to lend a hand to someone they know and trust.

On a deeper level, knowing someone creates a spiritual intimacy and a relational dynamic that is empowering. Think of the story of Jesus's encounter with the Samaritan woman in John 4:7-26. Jesus reaches across the barriers of gender and ethnic difference to engage the Woman at the Well in conversation. She is skeptical at first about why he is speaking with her. The turning point in the story occurs when the woman understands that Jesus knows everything about her and understands her personal situation. She goes on to proclaim him as Messiah and become an evangelist to her city, leading many others to Christ. Her relationship with Jesus was an empowering, synergistic relationship because Jesus took the time to speak with her and know her.

FORGING THE TIES THAT BIND

Because so many relationships develop organically, you may have never thought about deliberate steps you can take to broaden and deepen your network of relationships. But certain practices can help, particularly if your ministry context is large and complex or if you are new in your role.

The people who surround you are your mission field. They are potential co-workers in the vineyard of synergistic ministry. So it's important to pay attention to who's a part of your church, community, or ministry area. If your ministry is centered within the congregation, familiarize yourself with the membership roster and regular worship attenders. Get acquainted with key groups and stakeholders. If your ministry is centered in the community, take time to learn who's out there. Walk around the neighborhood. Seek out the official and unofficial community leaders. If you are already deeply invested in a particular community or ministry context, pay special attention to newcomers.

Learning someone's name is a critical first step in forging a relational bond. God's powerful claim on our lives flows from the fact that God searches us and knows us and calls us by name. Again and again in Scripture, whether it's the story of Moses or Jeremiah, Samuel or Saul of Tarsus, God broke through to them by calling them by name.

Adam Hamilton, pastor of the United Methodist Church of the Resurrection, describes how the congregation he started twenty-five years ago in a funeral home grew to be the largest United Methodist congregation. On Sunday afternoons, following services, Adam would drop by the home of each first-time worship visitor to deliver a coffee mug, thank them for attending worship, and invite them back the next Sunday. One benefit of these doorstep conversations was that Adam connected each visitor's name and face. If they returned the following Sunday, he could greet them by name. And this, more than anything else, says Adam, determined whether they would remain connected with the church.

Some people seem naturally gifted at remembering people's names. But in all likelihood, they've internalized certain practices that help them connect names with faces. For example, when I strike up a casual conversation with someone I don't know, I find that offering my name serves as an invitation for them to tell me theirs. "By the way, my name is Ann Michel. I'm not sure that we've met before." If they offer their name, I repeat it back immediately. "Jon Baker. I'm glad to know you, Jon." This helps cement the name in my memory. Simple mnemonic devices can also be helpful. A Tongan student named Siah introduced herself by telling me her name was pronounced like "See ya later," and I never forgot it. I also find it's helpful to jot down a new name as soon as possible following an introduction. You probably have some tricks of your own.

Taking the time to learn someone's name may seem simple or superficial, but we feel affirmed and valued when someone takes the time to learn and remember our name. It's an essential first step in building a meaningful relationship. So synergistic leaders apply themselves to the task of learning people's names.

Similarly, synergistic leaders make time to sit down regularly and have one-on-one conversations with people in the scope of their mission field for the sole purpose of getting to know them and finding out what makes them tick. We often think of Jesus surrounded by a crowd or in the midst of his band of disciples. But the Gospels also make clear that Jesus frequently took time to interact with people one-on-one, listening to them, hearing their stories, responding to their individual needs and circumstances. In casual conversation, we tend to stay with safe, superficial topics. But the aim of a relational meeting is to get beneath the surface by asking more probing questions. What drives you? Why do you do the things you do? What angers you? You might imagine that people would be put off by more probing conversation. But in fact, it honors and affirms their reality.

This type of dialogue can unleash core motivations and reveal clues about someone's gifts and calling. Listen carefully for clues that might help you direct another person into meaningful service or lead them into a new leadership role. Ask questions that will help them think about their talents and passions as evidence of where God is leading them. As disciples of Jesus, we are invited to "fish for people" (Matt 4:19 CEB). Relationships are the net that draws people in and connects them with Christ's body.

There are times when you need to meet with people for practical reasons—to ask them to do something, to coordinate activities, or to follow up on certain responsibilities. But these agendas have no place in a purely relational meeting. If you don't yet know the person, you have the perfect excuse to say "I'd like to get to know you better." If it's someone in the orbit of your ministry responsibility, say "I'd just like to touch base and see how things are going with you." Keep a running list of people you'd like to engage through relational meetings and set aside time for this important work.

The most gifted relational leaders I know are also deliberate about staying connected with people in their relational orbit. They pick up the phone just to check in and see how things are going. They drop by for a chat or suggest grabbing lunch or a cup of coffee. They are sincerely interested in knowing how you are doing. Various forms of electronic communication can be powerful tools in building and sustaining relationships. But there is growing evidence that the more we rely on our tablets, computer screens, and phones, the more isolated and adverse we become to more direct forms of communication. I used to think it absurd for people working within earshot of each other to send an e-mail or text rather than just speak to each other. But now it's the norm in my office. Days go by when my phone never rings because we've come to think of a phone conversation as an intrusion. We need to make sure that social media enhance our relationships, rather than supplanting them. This may explain why social media pioneer Mark Zuckerberg, the founder of Facebook, set a goal in 2014 to meet someone new every day. And his annual self-improvement goal for the following year was to extend a personal thank-you daily.[3]

For a long time, I'd been conditioned to think that there are task-oriented people who are good at getting things done and relationship-oriented people who prefer camaraderie to accomplishment. However, experience has taught me that nothing could be further from the truth. Relationships are essential to accomplishing all but the simplest of tasks. And sharing in the accomplishment of a mutual objective forges deep relational bonds. Task and relationship are not diametrically opposed. They are a mutually reinforcing element of synergy. The intrinsic strength of synergistic teamwork is that it unites task and relationship, making them two sides of the same coin.

Often, it's our own sense of self-importance that prevents us from investing fully in the potential of relationships. But relationality is a gift from God. As we embrace the relational nature of ministry, we reflect more fully the image of the triune God who created us. And we enter into the relational space that nurtures and propels synergy.

Discussion Questions

1. Think of a time when someone went out of his or her way to get to know you. How did it make you feel?

2. What are some reasons that people sometimes prefer to go it alone rather than investing in others?

3. Do you have personal practices that help you be more intentional about building and nurturing relationships?

4. Does the idea of being strategic about expanding your network of relationship seem insincere to you? Can you be both strategic and genuine in engaging others? How?

CHAPTER FIVE

Body Building

The Dynamics of Effective Team Ministry

Twenty-five years ago, my congregation created a small shelter for homeless men in our church building. We began to know our unhoused neighbors as individuals and as God's dearly loved children. This awareness shattered our stereotypes about homelessness. It transformed our attitudes. But the ministry was transformative in another sense as well. The impetus for the ministry didn't arise from the church's clergy or staff but from a committed group of lay persons seeking a meaningful response to the crisis of homelessness in our city. In creating our homeless ministry, one of our goals was to form a participatory, lay-driven leadership structure. The operation of the shelter would be managed by a group of volunteers, each with a specific, critical responsibility. Different people took the lead in different areas—coordinating overnight volunteers and meal donations, raising funds and soliciting supplies, maintaining the living space, working with a network of social workers to identify residents, and assisting residents as they transitioned out of the shelter.

As a young adult, relatively new to church leadership, the work was deeply formative for me. Spiritually, I came to understand how the Holy Spirit moves among us as we come together in common purpose. But there were practical lessons in the dynamics of church leadership too. Years later, when I became more familiar with leadership theory, I came to see how our homeless ministry plan embodied the key elements of effective team ministry. It was synergistic. So much so that twenty-five years later, the ministry still houses the homeless. Our program model has evolved in response to changing needs and standards of care. But our deep commitment to ministry among the homeless has not. And I believe this is in large part due to our commitment to team leadership.

In many, many congregations, teams provide hands-on, ongoing leadership for various projects or areas of ministry. Because working with others is an intrinsic aspect of ministry, all church leaders are called upon to work with teams—sometimes participating as a member of a team, sometimes facilitating a team's work, sometimes forming new teams, and sometimes coaching and advising others who form or facilitate teams. In reality, most of us are doing all these things all the time! Yet despite the ubiquity of leadership groups in congregational life, they are often constituted and coordinated in ways that fail to manifest the full potential of effective teamwork. Truly synergistic leaders master the dynamics of effective team ministry.

WHY TEAMS ARE IMPORTANT

Effective teams enhance the fruitfulness of ministry because they harness the power of synergy. When people work together effectively, they accomplish much more than they could on their own. Not only is more achieved but the work is more meaningful. Participants experience a sense of purpose, belonging, and fulfillment. Because good teamwork is rewarding and motivating, it facilitates individual growth and development.

Teams generate not only operational synergies but spiritual synergy as well. We grow as disciples by practicing discipleship, so the hands-on nature of team leadership is a catalyst of faith development. We are able to observe how other team members put their faith into action. And within the context of mutually supportive relationships, we can help each other explore the spiritual significance of our shared ministry. Everything we know about spiritual formation suggests that small-group encounters are important vehicles of growth. Ministry teams are often powerful incubators of faith because they provide necessary relational space and interpersonal bonding. If you have ever been on a mission trip, you have no doubt experienced how the team dynamic can foster spiritual exploration and discovery. Over the years, as part of a number of mission teams, I have witnessed amazing spiritual transformations. One individual came to Christ, another decided to join the church, another redirected her career path in order to better serve others, and yet another experienced the reawakening of a dormant call to ministry.

Teams can also expand the scope of a congregation's mission. According to George Barna, churches that deploy teams effectively are more likely to grow.[1] He maintains that people engaged in team leadership better understand the church's vision and are motivated to see it fulfilled. For this reason, their churches are "magnetic," says Barna, "invariably growing both numerically and spiritually."[2]

CHARACTERISTICS OF EFFECTIVE TEAMS

The term *team* is a buzzword in church leadership, so people sometimes call any collection of people doing just about anything a team. In reality, not every type of church group conforms to the technical definition of a team. *Ad hoc* groups focused on a short-term task, committees charged with studying issues or making recommendations, decision-making bodies, or small groups focused on fellowship, learning, and spiritual development, are not likely to exhibit all the characteristics that leadership theory ascribes to teams.[3] But don't get caught up on labels. In some congregations, every group is called a "committee" or a "small group" even if they are technically teams. And in other churches, every group is called a team, regardless of whether or not they function as one. The point in understanding the characteristics of effective teams isn't to split hairs or separate the sheep from the goats. Understanding the principles of effective team leadership can improve the function of all kinds of church groups.

Perhaps the most significant characteristic of teams is that they embody shared leadership. Effective teams do not have a single dominant leader surrounded by a group of subordinates. A team is a collection of leaders.[4] On truly high-functioning teams, there are no bystanders or onlookers. Everyone shares ownership in the responsibility and the outcomes, and everyone makes a contribution.[5]

For this reason, effective teams tend to be relatively small. Patrick Lencioni defines a team as three to twelve people who share common goals as well as rewards and responsibilities for achieving them.[6] The exact number isn't the point. But a team needs to be small enough that everyone matters. Everyone needs to be actively engaged.

When teams stay lean, members are more likely to get to know each other in a way that promotes mutual trust and collaboration. Everyone feels comfortable contributing to discussions, and every voice is heard. In larger groups debate tends to supplant dialogue, and it's more likely that a few dominant voices will prevail.

Because churches tend to place a high value on inclusiveness, they sometimes invite people to be part of teams even when they don't have much to contribute. That's a lovely gesture in a Sunday school class or a fellowship group. But on a team with serious leadership responsibilities, it can be a hindrance. Remember, Jesus cared for and related to a multitude of people. He had hundreds of followers. But only twelve were part of his leadership team.

Another critical factor in creating an environment of shared leadership is having distinct, differentiated roles for each member of the team. "For cooperation to succeed," according to leadership experts Jim Kouzes and Barry Posner, "tasks must be designed so that every person contributes something unique and independent to the final outcome. All individuals must clearly understand that unless they each contribute whatever they can, the team fails."[7] Motivation, buy-in, and accountability are enhanced when each team member knows the group's success depends on their efforts.

Think of a baseball team. The pitcher knows what he or she needs to do, and so does the catcher. They don't do the same thing. But each is important, and they rely on each other to play their part. Or recall once more Paul's teaching in 1 Corinthians 12, God's blueprint for synergistic teamwork: "The eye can't say to the hand, 'I don't need you,' or in turn, the head can't say to the feet, 'I don't need you.'" (1 Cor 12:21 CEB). The body of Christ, just like a human body, can only function properly when each of our organs does what it was designed to do. Members of Christ's body are united under the headship of Christ, and team members with different, distinct roles and complementary skills and abilities are united by a shared passion for their mission.

Job descriptions can be useful in clarifying the responsibilities of different team members, especially when launching a new team or recruiting new members onto an existing team. In my experience, though, even if you begin with a good division of labor, with the passage of time, some areas of responsibility may enlarge while others decline in importance. Or more proactive team members, usually with the best of intentions, take more on themselves than they should and end up eclipsing their teammates. So at certain junctures, you may need to rebalance the load. I've used an exercise I call a "task analysis" to form, and when necessary reform, team member responsibilities. It requires that you spend time brainstorming all the things that need to be done to accomplish your mission and then divide them into logical areas of responsibility. Successful teams tend to keep their focus narrow. So if the mission has expanded, or if the overall workload has grown too large for a reasonably sized team, subdivide the mission and start another team. This promotes the multiplication of ministry, increases active engagement, and contributes to church growth.

The idea of a team comprised of a group of leaders who share leadership begs the question: What then is the responsibility of the team's leader? It's certainly not to do the work on behalf of the group but rather to help facilitate and coordinate the work. Consider an orchestra director. He or she can't perform a symphony alone by merely reading a score and waving the baton. But without a conductor paying attention to how the different parts of the score come together and cuing the musicians when it's time for them to come in, the result would be a cacophony.

40

This image may be a bit overblown when we're talking about a small, collaborative group. But you get the idea! A good team leader also works to maintain the climate of the team itself—building and maintaining relationships, fostering bonds of fellowship and trust, attending to group dynamics in ways that support the ideal of shared leadership, and keeping the group focused on its mission.

BUILDING STRONG TEAMS

Whether your church already has a thriving culture of team leadership or teams are something new, getting the right people on a ministry team is a critical success factor. A strong team is comprised of individuals with complementary gifts and aptitudes united by a common passion for the mission.[8] On my homeless ministry team, for example, we have individuals with gifts of compassion, shepherding, giving, leadership, and administration brought together by our common concern for the homeless. In some church groups, such as a governing board, it's important that members represent different ages, interests, and constituent groups. But a ministry team is likely to be "unrepresentative," says Dan Hotchiss, an expert in church leadership structures. "The selection of ministry groups is based on people's passion for the goals, with an eye to making sure the group members have among them the gifts and time the ministry will need."[9]

When a team forms around an urgent, compelling mission, it's a magnet to those who care deeply about the cause. For this reason, healthy teams are generally able to perpetuate themselves. They know when they need to add someone new, and they are motivated to seek out the right individual. If a team struggles to

41

attract the needed participants, it may be that others don't find the cause compelling.

Trust is another critical success factor. You've probably been in church meetings where progress is stymied because people are unwilling to address openly the real issues at stake. People only name the elephants in the room when they trust one another enough to be completely honest, to express their opinions openly, and even to risk disagreeing with one another. For this reason, Patrick Lencioni maintains that trust is the vital foundation of all effective teamwork. A foundation of trust enables truly constructive engagement—legitimate give and take in which everyone feels safe to voice their opinions. This type of constructive engagement engenders commitment to the team itself and the decisions the team makes. When you feel your views have been heard, understood, and considered fairly, you are likely to support the group's decision even if it goes in a different direction from what you advocated. Trust fosters constructive engagement, and constructive engagement builds the emotional buy-in and commitment essential to a team's ability to fulfill its mission.[10]

Strong teams are intentional about maintaining this type of decision-making climate. They attend to building and strengthening relationships, fostering trust, and maintaining open and fully participatory communication. Developing a climate of trust takes time, but team-building activities that encourage interpersonal sharing and disclosure can jumpstart the process.[11] A team's relational bonds are also strengthened by setting aside time for social interaction, learning, prayer, and reflection. Jesus was a team builder. He selected disciples with diverse skills and backgrounds. He invested significant time in teaching and sharing a vision with them. He empowered them to serve while also providing feedback. And he encouraged them to withdraw on occasion from the crowd for spiritual renewal and prayer.

Strong ministry teams also attend to the spiritual dimension of their work, praying together regularly and engaging Scripture in more than token ways. They are deliberate about framing and expressing the spiritual significance of the team's work. They regularly lift up why what the team does matters to God, why it's important to the church's mission, and what it means to each team member's personal discipleship. In a spiritually mature group, this conversation might happen spontaneously. If not, the team leader will need to model the way, just as Jesus did.

Team leadership is the essence of synergy. But at the end of the day, our very humanness makes it difficult to embody this ideal fully. We are culturally conditioned to favor individual achievement and Lone-Ranger-style leaders. And all kinds of institutional pressures push back against team leadership. We want to know who's in charge. We imagine that having a single individual responsible for a job promotes efficiency, accountability, and control. We prefer clear lines of authority and leaving things to the experts. These proclivities explain in part why we in the church cling so dearly to the "father knows best" model of clergy leadership and why we default so readily to staff-driven programming. To realize the benefits of shared leadership, teams and their leaders must continually swim against this current. But working against resistance is a critical component of body building. And so it is, too, in building the body of Christ. Synergistic leaders invest energy in building and maintaining effective teams.

Discussion Questions

1. Think of a time when you've experienced teamwork at its best. What made it effective? Name some of the characteristics of the group experience.

2. Identify an existing team in your ministry setting. What's working, and what's not? How could its function be improved?

3. Identify a need or possibility for creating a new team. What steps might you take to form an effective team in response to this need?

CHAPTER SIX

Follow Me
The Art of Asking

T hink back to when you first got involved in church leadership. Maybe you woke up one morning and said, "Today, I'd
like to find something more to do. I wonder if I could take
on a church leadership role." Perhaps you read an inspiring article
in the church newsletter or heard a Sunday morning announcement so compelling you said, "That's for me! Where do I sign
up?" But if you are like the vast majority of people, you took the
first step because someone personally asked you to get involved.
Why do most church visitors attend a worship service? Because
they were invited. What's the biggest factor determining whether
people make gifts to support causes or ministries? Whether or not
they were solicited. How do most people decide to take on volunteer responsibilities? Because they were asked.

One of the primary responsibilities of any church leader is
to engage others in ministry. Much of your effectiveness will de-
pend on how well you do this, whether you are recruiting Sunday school teachers, amping up your praise team, or raising funds
to support youth ministry. Synergistic leaders master the art of
asking.

We all know what ineffective asking is like because it's so prevalent in the church. Someone puts out one blanket appeal after another. When the response is deafening silence, they get frustrated, possibly angry, that people are so indifferent to their cause. The appeals continue, but the tone becomes more desperate or negative, making them even less effective. Yet anyone can become accomplished in the art of asking by mastering the key elements of effective solicitation—whether seeking a commitment of someone's time or treasure.

A POSITIVE FRAME OF MIND

An appeal is most effective when offered in a bold, forthright, and confident manner. Yet some people seem to have an inherent level of personal discomfort when they approach the task of asking. At an emotional level, they're back on the high school dance floor, tongue-tied, awkward, and fearing rejection. I understand this emotional anxiety because I've been there. But then I realized I wasn't selling cars or magazine subscriptions. I was asking people to be part of something really important, so there was no need for embarrassment. If your ministry is important enough for you to devote your time, energy, and resources, why would you hesitate to ask someone else to join you? After all, regardless of your ministry focus, you are inviting people to be part of God's mission through the church.

If you're reticent about asking people to get involved in a ministry or to support it financially, think about these questions: Why is it important to you? Why is it important to them? And why is it important to God? Then practice articulating an ask that conveys this importance. Say it aloud until you can express it convincingly.

Even if the person you're asking can't respond positively, they'll come away from the encounter admiring your commitment.

Attaining the proper state of mind also means staying positive. Even if nine people decline your invitation to chair the hospitality team, you must approach the tenth person with just as much enthusiasm and grace as the first. It's tempting to fall back on appeals to guilt or obligation, but they motivate few, if any, people. Expressing desperation doesn't work either. It communicates that your ministry is struggling and marginal. No one wants to jump on board a project that is spiraling downward. People want to be part of something vibrant, exciting, and hopeful. Enthusiastic, positive asking will attract enthusiastic, positive people.

THE POWER OF PERSONAL INVITATIONS

Good fundraisers know that the most effective way to ask people for money is a face-to-face meeting. This is why personal visitation is the key element in any significant building campaign or major fund drive. Relationships matter. People are most motivated to support persons and organizations where they feel a connection.

Of course it isn't feasible to arrange a personal meeting every time you need to ask something of others. But a good rule in fundraising and recruiting is: the more personal the ask, the better. Yet many churches do most of their asking in the least personal, and therefore the least effective, ways: general announcements, newsletter articles, mass e-mails, and "dear friend" letters.

A relational ask is powerful because it can be framed around the individual's gifts, aptitudes, and interests. "Ashley, I've noticed how much you care about children and what a great Sunday school teacher you are. I think you'd enjoy the challenge of working with the new after-school tutoring program." Instead of the ask being framed around your need to find a volunteer, it's about how the opportunity can make a difference to the person you're asking. If you announce, "We need *somebody* to work with the after-school program," the busy person thinks, "Thank goodness it doesn't need to be me." The uncertain person thinks, "They can't mean me." But when you ask someone personally, it says, "This isn't a role for just *anybody*." The person you're asking thinks, "I must have something unique to offer."

MAKE IT EASY TO SAY YES

Never ask something of people without making it clear and obvious how they can respond to your request. An effective ask has a built-in response mechanism. Lots of pulpit announcements fail because there is no immediate way to respond. If you ask people to call the church office to register for the new Lenten study, your ask assumes an interested person will remember your request and act on it later when their phone is in hand and the church office is open. It leaves a lot to chance. When you make a request of people in the pews, give them an immediate way to respond—perhaps a registration card or a tear-off form in the bulletin to place in the offering plate. If passing a sign-up sheet isn't too disruptive to your style of worship, it allows people to commit on the spot. And it might even create a bit of positive peer pressure.

If you have a personal meeting with a prospective donor or volunteer and they want time to think about your request, do not put the responsibility on them to get back to you. Say, "I'm glad you're willing to consider this. Would it be okay if I get back in touch with you next week?" And then make sure you do. If you send an e-mail requesting that people sign up for an activity or make a monetary donation, provide a link so that people can respond immediately online. If you request something by mail, include a preaddressed return envelope, preferably postage-paid.

It's also important to honor those whose answer is no. No matter how effective your asking, some people have valid reasons they can't respond to your request. So an artful asker knows how to gracefully receive no as an answer. If you do not create space for people to honestly decline your invitations, they will eventually start dodging your questions. If someone's reply is an honest, thoughtful no, you have gained valuable information to help you approach them the next time with something more fitting. Moreover, no doesn't always mean no. Sometimes people's initial response is no because they need more time to think about the request. I've been surprised, over and over again, particularly in fundraising, to find that people who initially said no eventually responded affirmatively.

AIM HIGH AND CAST A WIDE NET

You never know until you've asked! This is why a lot of seasoned fundraisers are not shy about asking for large amounts of money. Asking something significant of someone creates a positive dynamic. It communicates that you think the person is capable of doing something important. And if they can't respond positively to your initial request, you have created space to discuss other options. If your prospect says, "I'm afraid giving $10,000 just isn't an option for me at this stage of life," you can respond, "I certainly understand. Would a $3,000 gift be more reasonable?"

You've honored their reality while still allowing them to support your cause.

I've found the same dynamic exists when recruiting volunteers. Some people I've asked to head up a project or team will say, "I'm not sure I can take on the leadership, but I'd be glad to be part of the group." I always view this as a win, not only because I've recruited a strong team member but also because I can tell the next person I approach about chairing the effort that a great team is already coming together.

Because assembling a team can require this type of creative back and forth, I always start by casting a wide net. Don't assume there's only one person who can do the job. I begin any significant recruiting effort by looking over the entire church roster. It always helps me think of some people who might not otherwise come to mind. It keeps me from relying on a small group of usual suspects.

It's also helpful to mix it up occasionally. There are some asks that need to be made over and over again. In operating the homeless shelter at my church, for example, we are continually asking people to donate meals and volunteer. Over the years, we have had several different systems for recruiting volunteers. First, it was a big sign-up calendar in the church social hall, then phone-a-thons. Later e-mail provided a convenient way to reach people, and eventually we set up an online volunteer calendar. Each time we adopted a new approach, the initial response was strong. We were sure we had finally discovered the best system for recruiting volunteers. But eventually, the response to each of these systems would taper off. There is usually no one best way of asking people to serve. Some people respond better to one approach and others to something different. I have found this also true of new member systems and annual stewardship drives. Trying something different and keeping it fresh generally yields positive results.

GRATITUDE AND SINCERITY

Effective asking is supported by two other interrelated forms of communication. In his book *Ask, Thank, Tell,* Charles R. Lane describes an ongoing cycle of communication in which asking is connected to thanking people and telling the story of what a ministry accomplishes.[1] Generally, we put most of our emphasis on asking, but asking is more effective when supported by these other motivating elements. An effective ask always begins by thanking people for what they have already done. An effective thank-you tells the story of what someone's involvement or contribution has made possible. And this creates a positive climate for another ask.

I know many leaders who set aside time weekly to thank volunteers or donors whose support is critical to their ministry goals. They make a regular practice of jotting off a few handwritten thank-you notes or making a few phone calls to express appreciation. This isn't only a good strategy for maintaining engagement, it helps cultivate the mind-set of gratitude that is essential to servant leadership.

Much of our credibility when we ask things of others comes by virtue of our own willingness to serve and sacrifice. I'm most motivated to help those people whose commitment and service I respect. For this reason, I've always observed a simple rule: I don't ask someone else to do something I wouldn't be willing to do myself. While the techniques and strategies of effective asking are important, at the end of the day they must be grounded in gratitude, clarity of purpose, and sincerity. This is at the heart of synergistic leadership.

Discussion Questions

1. Do you ever feel awkward about asking people to do things? If so why? What would help you approach the task more enthusiastically?

2. Recall a time when you've been invited to do something in a way that made you want to do it.

3. Think of some of the less-than-effective ways your church tries to appeal to people. How might you reframe or improve the ask?

CHAPTER SEVEN

Two by Two

Developing Others as Leaders

Synergistic leadership is never about accumulating power and influence for oneself. Synergistic leaders are continually giving leadership away by identifying new leaders and helping them grow. The synergy that propelled the growth of the early church was grounded in Jesus's dedication to replicating and multiplying the leadership of his movement.[1] The vitality of our ministries is intrinsically related to our effectiveness in raising up new leaders.

FORMAL AND INFORMAL LEADERSHIP DEVELOPMENT

Most congregations have structures and processes aimed at moving people into leadership roles, such as nominating committees, leadership training events, job descriptions, recruitment drives, and so forth. This institutional infrastructure constitutes a congregation's formal leadership development system. But in healthy, vital congregations, leaders are being nurtured in organic ways as well. A congregation's informal leadership development system often revolves around existing leaders who are relationally connected to others and attuned to their gifts and passions.

They invite potential new leaders to come alongside them and to learn through experience, on-the-job training, and informal mentoring.

Ideally, a church's formal and informal leadership development systems reinforce one another. An effective formal system augments and reinforces a healthy culture of organic leadership growth, but it's rarely sufficient unto itself. Unless it's undergirded and fed by new people bubbling up through informal leadership cultivation, a nominating process and other formal structures will either recycle the same old people into different roles or rush new people into leadership before they are ready. In many declining churches, the formal, institutional systems still operate, but they have run out of gas because no new energy is coming into the system. When confronted with leadership needs, these churches tend to schedule generic leadership training events or Bible studies, or send people off to denominational training events. But these programmatic responses generally fail absent a meaningful investment in personal relationships.[2]

Leadership doesn't develop in a vacuum. The motivation to lead emerges as one becomes more and more deeply invested in a particular mission and the people connected to it. Leaders are developed on the way toward something else. This is one reason I've never put much credence in the common advice that congregations should look for new leaders among their spiritually mature people who have demonstrated their commitment through measures such as tithing and faithful worship attendance. As important as these things are, I've yet to find (in my church at least) that group of spiritually mature tithers sitting on the back bench waiting to be invited into leadership. In my experience, it works the opposite way. People grow in faith and commitment as they become deeply invested in the mission of the church. This was certainly true of Jesus's disciples, whose spiritual shortcomings are well documented in the Gospels. If Jesus had been looking for disciples who already manifested compliance with the expectations of the faith, he might have looked to the Pharisees. Instead, he called an unlikely band of followers, knowing that their shared ministry would be the fulcrum of faith formation and leadership growth. Involving people in ways that move them simultaneously toward deeper faith and widening leadership engagement is an important facet of synergy.

ORGANIC LEADERSHIP DEVELOPMENT

The organic approach to leadership development is reflected in the story of one church leader working to get others involved in a ministry of visitation with shut-ins. He would first invite a new person to come along with him to visit a particular shut-in. The new person was introduced but mainly observed the visit. The next time he visited that shut-in, the new person was again invited to come along and, this time, was encouraged to join fully in the conversation. The next time, the new visitor was asked to initiate the contact and take the lead in the conversation. By the forth visit, the new person was doing everything, with the seasoned leader just there to provide support and smile a lot. Following each visit, the two debriefed over lunch. And after these four visits, the new person knew how to do a really good home or hospital visit. Even better, they had learned how to teach and coach the next new person coming into this ministry.[3]

This relatively simple process mirrors the pattern of how Jesus engaged others in his ministry. Leadership experts observe this four-step progression of leadership development in the Gospels: First, Jesus does something. Next, he does it with the disciples observing. Then, the disciples do it, but Jesus is with them. And finally, the disciples do it themselves.[4] Another leadership development strategy Jesus employed was pairing leaders together. In Luke's Gospel we read that when Jesus appointed seventy others,[5] sending them out ahead of him to proclaim God's kingdom, he sent them out in pairs, two by two (Luke 10:1). Before sending them on their mission, Jesus instructs them carefully. And following their work, they return to Jesus to debrief, celebrate, and give thanks to God.

We are often so eager to get new people to take on responsibilities that we short-circuit this process. We hand off a responsibility to someone else and expect them to do it on their own, without devoting time to the intermediate steps that teach them and bring them along. But when organic, relational leadership development is part of a church's culture, leadership becomes self-replicating. It drives synergy and synergistic growth, just as it did in the New Testament church.

This approach is so simple and intuitive that anyone can do it, if you are willing to invest yourself in bringing someone else along. For example, whenever someone asks me to lead a Bible study, I say, "I'll do it if you're willing to serve as co-leader." This works particularly well with a structured curriculum, such as an in-depth Bible study over several months. I insist that we take turns leading the weekly sessions, and when it's my partner's turn, I participate in the lesson along with the other members of the group. By the end of the year, my co-leader has enough experience and confidence to team with someone else new.

One church in Washington, DC, was constantly struggling to recruit enough Sunday school teachers. They came up with a counterintuitive strategy. Instead of recruiting a single teacher for each classroom, they recruited a team of four. Paradoxically, instead of magnifying their recruiting challenges, it resolved them. People were much more willing to say yes when they knew there were others to share the responsibility. One result was a much larger, more reliable stable of teachers. But even more importantly, the change resulted in enhanced camaraderie and creative problem-solving that deepened each teacher's commitment to the shared ministry.[6] Leaders are more likely to grow when they work together.

MUTUAL MENTORING AND SHARED LEADERSHIP

One challenge when working with new leaders is helping them learn the ropes without insisting that they do things exactly the way you do them. Younger leaders often complain of older folks in churches who are eager for them to step up and help shoulder the burdens of running the church but just as quick to slap them down if they do not do things just as their elders did. An advantage of the relational approach to leadership development is that it allows for mutual mentoring—seasoned leaders and new leaders learning from each other. In his book *A Work of Heart: Understanding How God Shapes Spiritual Leaders*, Reggie McNeal examines how God shaped Moses, David, Jesus, and Paul as leaders, primarily through their experiences and interactions within their communities. Jesus and his disciples functioned as a mutual learning community. Not only did Jesus shape the community of disciples but the disciples helped shape Jesus as a leader, serving collectively as a sounding board and a feedback loop that helped Jesus understand his mission field and evaluate the impact of his ministry.[7]

Sharing leadership requires a willingness to cede control and be open to new ideas and insights. Making space for someone else to grow is a self-sacrificial gesture of servant leadership. It communicates that "it's not all about me." It is important to remember that God has already empowered and uniquely gifted each of us for ministry. Our role in developing other leaders is to help them claim the call to lead that is incumbent in what God has already done.

The organic approach to leadership development draws together many aspects of synergistic leadership previously discussed: the importance of relationships, the power of personal invitations, and the generative nature of team leadership. But synergy becomes an even more potent force when these elements come together in a way that gives rise to new leaders. The multiplication of leadership has an exponential impact on the reach of a church's ministries. And new leaders breathe new life into a congregation. Renewal of the church today depends on our ability to reclaim this critical element of synergy.

Discussion Questions

1. Can you think of a time when someone took you under their wing to help you grow as a leader? What was notable or important about that experience?

2. In your church, is more attention given to formal or informal leadership development systems?

3. Read Luke 10:1-24. What do you observe about the way Jesus equipped his disciples as leaders?

4. Can you think of a time when others have been reluctant to share leadership with you? Or when you have been reluctant to share leadership with others? What might have made it easier?

5. What are some simple first steps you might take to help new leaders get engaged?

Where Two or More Are Gathered

Mastering Meetings

A clergy friend, as he headed into his umpteenth meeting of the week, joked, "Have you heard the one about the pastor who died and went to heaven? His tombstone read, 'He never has to attend another meeting.' " I replied, only half-jokingly, "What do you think the saints are doing in glory?" If we really believe Christ's promise "Where two or three are gathered in my name, I'm there with them" (Matt 18:20 CEB), then our meetings should be holy ground—places where the Holy Spirit can act among us because the people of God have gathered in common purpose. Yet most church leaders dread meetings because they are so often boring, frustrating, and unproductive. But synergistic leaders understand that meetings can and should be positive, productive venues for advancing God's mission through the church. They learn how to master meetings.

HAVE YOU BEEN TO A MEETING LIKE THIS?

The worship team at Grace Church always meets the third Thursday of the month at seven o'clock. On the appointed evening, a little after 7:00 p.m., members start drifting into their meeting room, chatting as they wait for the team leader, Sam. Because he comes straight from his office, Sam often runs a bit late and is sometimes a little harried when he arrives. When he finally gets there, he's drawn into the small talk but eventually calls the group together saying, "What do we need to talk about this month?"

Sarah, the choir director, jumps right in proudly reading through a long list of hymns and anthems for the next two months. Most team members are not particularly interested in all the specifics. Those who are interested wonder why she had not merely handed out a list. Jim, the leader of the praise band, then takes the floor. He says he feels a Saturday night service would be more attractive to younger people, and he asks the team to formally endorse the creation of this new worship service. Since this idea had never been discussed before, everyone is caught off guard. Soon, the conversation gets heated as people express opinions about different styles of worship music. Jim calls for a vote. Others complain there's no consensus. Sam isn't sure how to proceed. Finally, someone has the presence of mind to suggest deferring the issue for the time being.

Ellen, the head of the altar guild, immediately launches into a series of complaints about people moving things in the chancel and not putting them away properly. By 8:30 p.m., people are looking at their watches and getting fidgety. Team leader Sam appears to be bringing the meeting to a close. But as people start to get up, he says, "Before we go home, there's one thing I forgot to share. The Finance Committee is asking every ministry area to trim its budget by 3 percent, and we need to come up with a plan."

The already-tired group doesn't take this news well. First there's some grumbling, then some random suggestions, but after thirty minutes, there's no progress on formulating a plan. Some people are slipping out the back door due to the lateness of the hour. Eager to bring the meeting to a close, Sam asks for volunteers to work up a plan before the next meeting. Somewhat reluctantly, three team members raise their hands, mostly because they're ready to go home. But Sam dismisses the group without specifying who would be responsible for calling this subgroup together. The next time the group meets, no one can remember who had agreed to do what. And they still have no budget plan.

I've endured countless meetings like this one, and you probably have too. But many of the common pitfalls that tripped up this group can be avoided by adhering to some simple best practices. While much of the responsibility for making a meeting work falls to the chair or team leader, every church leader can contribute to a productive, synergistic group dynamic.

PURPOSEFUL MEETINGS

The essential foundation of an effective meeting is clarity about what the meeting needs to accomplish. Leadership expert Stephen R. Covey calls this "beginning with the end in mind."[1] Lovett Weems would say you need to know your "so that."[2] "Our worship team will meet this month *so that* we can finalize the elements of our Sunday services during Lent." Or, in the case of the Grace Church worship team, "Our team is meeting this month *so that* we can formulate a plan to trim our budget." Every time you call a group together you should be clear about the objective of the gathering.

The corollary of this is: don't meet just to meet. Some groups may need standing meetings. But many probably do not. If a group is meeting largely because the members enjoy getting together, then it's become a social group. There's nothing wrong with a social group, if that's the group's purpose. But if the social group is supposed to be the worship team, it's hard to explain to someone new why so much time is spent visiting. All good groups have a social dimension. But it shouldn't overtake its primary focus. Make sure every time you meet it's for a legitimate purpose.

Once you're clear about the purpose of your meeting, a well-crafted agenda is the next critical element. Sam's meeting got off on the wrong foot and never recovered in part because he had no agenda. But a productive meeting requires more than just *having* an agenda. Marching a group through an opening prayer, minutes, old business, and new business usually won't provide enough structure to support your group's work. You need a *good* agenda. And a good agenda is a game plan for how the meeting will accomplish its purpose. Sam should have crafted his agenda to help the group process the budget decision.

Crafting an effective game plan for your meeting requires forethought and advance preparation. What information is relevant to the discussion? What key questions will help the group think through the relevant issues? Who needs to be at the table? It often means you need to consult in advance with key members of the group or other groups to shape your agenda. But a word of caution is in order here. As you become more deliberate about advance planning, it's possible to get so far out in front of your group that you forget how much time it can take for them to process issues.

MAXIMIZE PARTICIPATION

Meetings are dreadfully boring for attendees when they're placed in a passive role. Sometimes, they're forced to listen to endless reports. Or they're expected to listen and nod as the person running the meeting presents a preformulated plan for their approval. And sometimes a meeting chair will try to control the outcome or avoid conflict by keeping a tight lid on conversation. The consequence of dull meetings is more than just a few yawns or nodding heads. Meeting participants lulled into boredom are unlikely to surface all the issues and concerns that need to be brought to the table. The consequence can be poor decisions.[3] Moreover, those who have not engaged actively in discussion and decision-making are less committed to the outcome, so any consensus achieved is fragile. Lively and participatory meetings are not just more entertaining, they are a fulcrum of participatory, synergistic energy.

Some simple strategies can help. Begin by building your agenda around some well-framed discussion questions. This alone signals that you are open to input and ideas. And allow enough time for open discussion before moving too quickly to solutions.[4] This gives everyone a chance to internalize the issues at hand.

As conversation takes shape, be deliberate about drawing less active people into the discussion. It often takes just a bit of polite encouragement to get the more hesitant to speak. "Andrew, you look like you have something to say." Or, "Rachel, we haven't heard from you yet. What do you think?" You can gently remind the more dominant speakers that others need to be heard by saying, "Josh, thanks for sharing your perspective. Let's hear from some others now." The good news is, if you direct people in these ways often enough, they may eventually internalize the norm of sharing air space and monitor their own levels of participation.

In larger groups, it's generally helpful to break into smaller conversation clusters for portions of the meeting. This can be done very simply by saying, "Let's each turn to the person sitting next to us to discuss the next question on the agenda." I find it's usually unnecessary, and often a little tedious, to follow this by asking each group to report on their smaller conversations. It's usually sufficient to say, "Is there anything you want to share with the larger group?"

KEEP REASONABLE TIME LIMITS

It's difficult to sustain people's attention over long periods of time, so regular team or committee meetings are best kept to ninety minutes or two hours, at the most. It's incumbent on whoever is chairing a meeting to monitor the use of time and keep things moving toward a conclusion, or find acceptable ways of leaving things off. The simple discipline of starting and ending on time reinforces good stewardship of time. If you delay the opening of a meeting until all latecomers arrive, it rewards the tardy and gives permission to everyone to come late the next time. In formulating an agenda, be realistic about the length of time it will take for a group to handle the business at hand. It's better to spread the work over several meetings than frustrate a group with an overly ambitious meeting plan.

Meetings often become long and boring when reports and information sharing crowd out active discussion and decision-making. One of the quickest ways to lose control of a meeting is to open the floor to anyone who has something to say or circle around the table letting people bring up whatever they want. It's important to present information in efficient and succinct ways.

Some groups ask members to provide all updates in writing in advance of the meeting. This is a wonderful idea if your group buys into it. In my church it has never worked well. People are too busy to meet the deadline for submitting their reports. And they're too busy to take time to read them before the meeting. But more to the point, I think most people want the affirmation of having their work brought to the attention of the whole team. One way to honor this dynamic is to take turns. Instead of having everyone report at each meeting, schedule their reports over several different meetings. This gives each group their time in the spotlight and encourages them to be a bit more prepared and creative when it's their turn.

Something as simple as leaving reports until the end of the meetings can prevent them gobbling up too much time. Commonly, reports are listed at the beginning of an agenda. But if the reporting goes long, the action items are short-changed. Putting program updates or need-to-know notices last on the agenda really encourages brevity.

ALLOW SPACE FOR THE SPIRIT TO WORK

Often the way we do church meetings is heavily influenced by secular decision-making paradigms, whether it's our understanding of the democratic process or the way meetings are conducted in the workplace. Those who have honed their group process skills in secular settings can be a tremendous asset to their church groups. But too often, the only difference between our church meetings and workplace meetings is a brief opening or closing prayer. I've attended plenty of meetings where somebody says a perfectly nice little prayer at the beginning and somebody prays for traveling mercies at the end, or the pastor is invited to "pray the group out," but the meeting that occurs between these spiritual bookends is unaffected.

Synergistic leaders find ways to infuse their meetings with spiritual energy. In the midst of a group's deliberations, they ask, "Where do you see the Spirit's presence in this discussion?" They seek the Spirit's guidance when the group must deal with difficult issues. They take time to pray in the face of disagreement or uncertainty. They frame issues with relevant Bible study. If group leaders do not model this type of spiritual inquiry, others will easily fall back on secular decision-making norms. Yet at the same time, you want to avoid fostering the assumption that bringing a spiritual perspective is something only a leader, staffer, or clergyperson can do.

COMING TO A DECISION

Perhaps the most critical meeting management skill is helping a group come to a decision. So you need to listen carefully to the drift of the conversation and be attentive to threads of agreement. It can be helpful at key junctures simply to name where you hear commonalities. "I've heard a number of you suggest that we should postpone the start of Vacation Bible School until after the Fourth of July. Is this something we are agreed on?"

Smaller teams and groups generally don't make decisions by vote, but calling for a quick vote can be an expeditious way of moving forward if a consensus is apparent. If you're not sure whether a decision has emerged, a quick, nonbinding straw poll can reveal where things stand. In a small group, this can also be accomplished by simply circling around the table and asking people what they think should be done. When I employ these techniques I'm generally surprised to find there is more consensus than I think, perhaps because debate tends to center around objections, even if they are not held by the majority present.

You don't necessarily need unanimity to move forward. Waiting until each and every person is in complete agreement can cause frustration or paralysis. Patrick Lencioni says people will buy into a group's decision as long as they feel their ideas were heard, understood, and considered. Good leaders drive commitment by extracting all opinions, ideas, and views, and then having the courage to move ahead.[5]

Finally, while following *Robert's Rules of Order* generally leads to a stilted, formal meeting, I have witnessed situations where the *Rules of Order* have been used to rein in a meeting that had gotten out of hand. So it never hurts to be prepared to fall back on sound parliamentary procedure if it becomes necessary.

MONITOR FOLLOW-THROUGH

You can have the best meeting ever, but if nothing comes of it after people leave the room, they will still end up feeling that the meeting was a waste of their time. So synergistic leaders take steps to assure that their plans come to fruition. People need clarity in order to take action. So never leave a meeting room without clarifying exactly what was decided. As a meeting comes to a close, review what you've agreed to and ask, "What exactly have we decided today?"[6]

Another simple method of enabling follow-through is to put together a written summary of the meeting. Some groups may need to record formal minutes, but most groups or teams need only a summary of actions steps that constitute a group to-do list. Here is an example of a written meeting summary for a team:

- The children's ministry team decided to postpone the start of Vacation Bible School until after the Fourth of July.

- Susan will confirm the availability of classrooms the week of July 11.

- Richard will draft an announcement for the church newsletter.

- Emily will identify a new music leader since Ian isn't in town the week of July 11.

- Pat will double-check the availability of teachers and locate replacements if necessary. She will also order the curriculum.

- Mary will inventory supplies left over from last year and order what's needed.

- Rachel will come up with a publicity plan for community outreach and share it at the next team meeting.

- The group agreed to meet again on April 27 at 6 p.m.

It's best to send this summary within twenty-four hours of the meeting's adjournment, while discussions are still fresh in people's minds. Having this type of meeting summary in hand the next time the group meets keeps everyone accountable to their commitments.

Another accountability tool is a dashboard or other metrics that track a group's progress on overarching goals. The children's ministry team might, for example, want to monitor statistics on Sunday school attendance, attendance at other children's events, the participation of leaders and teachers, the number of new families reached, and so on.

An effective church meeting is never an end unto itself. It's an instrument of effective ministry. But well-run, participatory, Spirit-filled meetings can help generate synergy by setting the stage for meaningful action. Effective leaders learn how to master meetings.

Discussion Questions

1. What is your experience with meetings? Do you find them boring and frustrating? Or purposeful and spirited? What accounts for this experience?

2. Think of some times when you were in a meeting that went off the tracks. What strategies might help keep a meeting on course?

3. How might you approach meetings in a way that would make them more Spirit-filled?

4. Take a moment to think about an upcoming meeting. What is the hoped-for objective? Jot down some ideas for an agenda that would help accomplish its objective.

CHAPTER NINE

Quick to Hear, Slow to Speak and Anger

Dealing with Conflicts and Complaints

I t's often said that a church with no conflict is a dead church. And up to a point, that is true. But it's also true that petty conflicts and complaints create unnecessary friction and unpleasantness, impeding synergy. Unresolved differences and difficulties can metastasize into systemic conflict that erodes the relational ties that undergird synergy, rendering a congregation toxic and dysfunctional. Each year an estimated 10 percent of churches face conflict serious enough to require special action or outside remediation.[1] For this reason, synergistic leaders are strategic about how they engage conflict.

Conflict has a way of hooking us because it triggers our emotions rather than our intellect. An organizational psychologist helped me understand that this is hardwired into our brain function. When confronted with a complaint or allegation, our brain perceives it as a threat. The stimulus is channeled into the primitive part of our brain responsible for flight-or-fight responses, bypassing the part of the brain responsible for rational decision-making.

No wonder we are so prone to overreact, respond emotionally, and blow things out of proportion!

Additionally, many of us have ingrained habits when it comes to dealing with conflict. By disposition, some of us are inherently conflict-averse while others thrive on controversy. And many of us have a default setting defined by our family of origin or our cultural background. For example, I grew up in a family where no one ever—I mean *ever*—raised their voice. As a consequence, any time a conversation gets a bit heated or animated, to my ears, it sounds like yelling, and my emotional triggers are activated. This part of me wants to avoid conflict. But I am also quite passionate about ideas and have strongly held beliefs. So when something I care about is at stake, I can be like a dog with a bone. Trained as an intercollegiate debater, I am not afraid to argue anybody down in public. I used to think it paradoxical that I am both conflict-averse and confrontational, but as I learned more about conflict management, I discovered this is a somewhat common profile. This shows that my default setting is to stay within myself rather than seek more interactive ways of dealing with conflict. If you do an Internet search for "conflict resolution" or "conflict management," you will come across a number of online questionnaires and quizzes that can help you identify your own default setting for dealing with conflict.

CHOOSE YOUR BATTLES

The instinctive ways we tend to respond to differences or disagreements are not always the best ways. Savvy, experienced leaders master a range of different responses to conflict and are strategic about deciding which is appropriate in a given situation.

Many leadership theorists use a schema to depict a range of possible responses to conflict, charting them according to the assertiveness of the response and the degree of cooperation required. The diagram below illustrates five possible responses: avoidance, accommodation, compromise, confrontation, and collaboration.

Possible Responses to Conflict

This diagram shows that avoidance and accommodation are low in terms of the degree of assertiveness or effort required, while confrontation and collaboration are high on that scale. Accommodation and collaboration involve more engagement with the perspective of the other party in a dispute than do avoidance or confrontation. Compromise is at the midpoint on both scales. While many leadership experts use these categories, I am indebted to Norma Cook Everist's discussion in *Church Conflict: From Contention to Collaboration*.[2] Many of the points that follow are drawn from her analysis.

Avoidance. Some regard avoiding conflict as an unhealthy form of denial or passive-aggressive behavior. But there are times when deciding not to engage a particular controversy is the most appropriate response. When the stakes are low, when your attention is more needed elsewhere, when you need to buy time or gather information, or when there is an overriding need to keep the peace, the best response to a problem may be to find a graceful way to side-step or postpone the issue.

Accommodation. Similarly, accommodating those with whom you disagree is often regarded as a weak or passive posture. But yielding in favor of a different point of view can sometimes be the most gracious and appropriate thing to do, particularly when maintaining a good relationship with the other party is more important than the outcome of a particular debate. So strategic leaders know when it's most advantageous to give way and simply let others have their way.

Confrontation. There are also times when it's best to deal with an issue head on, debate it out, and make an up-or-down decision. This may involve taking a dispute public or bringing the issue before relevant decision-making authorities. Taken to its extreme, confrontation can put the outcome of the decision at risk. It can also risk alienating others and escalating tensions, unless the debate occurs in a forum with agreed-upon ground rules and within an overall environment of trust. The most appropriate times for confrontation are when very important issues or principles are at stake that can't be compromised or when a decision can't be delayed.

Compromise. Often, when faced with differences, we will choose to compromise by agreeing to split the difference, with each party making a concession to find a mutually acceptable middle ground in order to move on. Strategically, compromise is somewhere between confrontation and accommodation, at the midpoint on the scales of assertiveness and collaboration. Compromise is often an expedient and fair way to move forward. But because the outcome is less than ideal for everyone, it's never the perfect solution.

Collaboration. At times it's desirable to work together to resolve an issue in a mutually satisfactory way, finding a creative win-win solution that fully satisfies the concerns of both parties without the sacrifices involved in compromise. While this type of collaborative work may seem like the ideal way to deal with all differences, it takes a great deal of time and energy and a high degree of relational investment. So collaboration isn't a practical response to every situation. When the stakes are low, or when there isn't a mutual commitment to finding a solution, it can be more expedient to avoid, accommodate, or compromise.

The key is to understand that there's not one right way of engaging conflict. There are times when it's appropriate to avoid conflict or accommodate those with whom you differ, and other times when it's appropriate to confront a situation openly. Some situations call for compromise and others collaboration. Synergistic leaders understand that each of these strategies needs to be in their repertoire of conflict management stills. And they need to intentionally cultivate the self-awareness and emotional discipline needed to be strategic about engaging conflicts in the most appropriate ways.

Just like every other church leader, I've had to deal with my fair share of complaints from other members of the church. I've also had the unhappy experience of working in a congregation that was deeply divided by a personnel conflict. I've learned a lot of lessons the hard way. I've made a lot of mistakes. And like everyone else, I continue to make mistakes. But in the back-and-forth of congregational life, I've stumbled upon a few key principles that I have found to be best practices for dealing with conflicts.

ASSUME THE BEST OF OTHERS

Once, as part of the stewardship team in my church, I was helping organize a series of gatherings in our pastor's home to discuss the church's vision. After receiving an invitation to one of these events, a long-time church member expressed anger that her adult son had not been invited. She accused the stewardship team of failing to invite him because he didn't have the means to support the church financially. In fact, her son was on the invitation list for a gathering for other younger adults, and his invitation was quite literally in the mail. On hearing her complaint, my first response was annoyance. What business did this woman have challenging the stewardship team's carefully designed outreach plan? But I was also inwardly gleeful because I knew she was wrong and I was right about the facts of the matter. And nothing would have given me more emotional satisfaction than telling her so. But instead of becoming defensive, I took a deep breath, and before explaining the situation, I said this: "Marilyn, I totally understand why you're concerned about your son being included. Nothing is more important to me as a mother than seeing my children fully engaged in the life of the church, so I get where you're coming from." With this, her anger just evaporated. She said, "You're right. I guess I just can't stop being a mom. I'm so glad you understand." I avoided an argument and left Marilyn feeling affirmed rather than belittled.

To use the terminology of my colleague Lovett Weems, this is a way of approaching a situation with "a presumption of grace" rather than a "presumption of judgment." We all have a natural tendency to assume the worst of other people, particularly when we find ourselves at odds with them for some reason. So it's important to consider things from the other person's point of view, thinking about what's driving them and what deeper values may be involved. This is, of course, easier said than done, especially in the midst of a disagreement. But part of maturing and growing as a leader is cultivating the self-awareness to approach difficult situations in a more objective way.

TALK TO PEOPLE INSTEAD OF ABOUT THEM

Imagine a situation where you're angry with Mike, the editor of your church's newsletter, because he never gets the publication out on schedule. It would be most logical to discuss the problem directly with Mike. But that is rarely how we deal with such problems in churches or other complex social systems. You don't particularly want to get into an uncomfortable conversation with Mike. So instead, you complain to the pastor, thinking that she will share your concern. After all, doesn't the pastor have more authority over the newsletter editor than you do? And isn't it likely that the pastor will share your concern? After talking to the pastor, you end up feeling a bit better. You've avoided having to confront Mike. And you assume the pastor will take up your cause with him. But in reality, the pastor is no more eager to raise a problem with Mike than you are. In fact, she's got a lot at stake in her relationship with Mike. So rather than doing your bidding, she is vague with Mike, saying, "Some people are a little worried about the newsletter schedule, but it will probably blow over." In the end, Mike doesn't even realize there's a problem that needs to be addressed. You end up wondering why the newsletter still isn't being sent out on time, and the pastor has put herself in an awkward position.[3]

Systems theorists call this pattern of conflict avoidance "triangulation." When larger or more emotionally charged issues are involved, more and more third parties get triangulated into problems, and conflict can spread like wildfire. This type of behavior is a normal mechanism for covering over differences and minimizing the anxiety that comes with conflict. But it also explains how conflicts can spread so quickly, why issues can get so murky and muddled, and why the real problems seldom get addressed. The end product is generally confusion and distrust.[4] To avoid these pitfalls, we need to step away from the pattern of talking *about* someone with whom we have a problem, and instead deal directly *with* that individual. And when someone else tries to triangulate you into a dispute you're not a party to, you need to be able to say, "I don't really need to be involved in this. It seems like you should take it up directly with Mike."

AVOID RESPONDING TO COMPLAINTS BY E-MAIL

In her book *Real Good Church*, Molly Phinney Baskette describes a scenario that is all too familiar to most church leaders: "You receive an e-mail and the subject line says 'A concern.' And you have to scroll down five times to read the entire length of the e-mail. You get mad, then you get sad, then you spend two hours crafting your carefully written response. Then they send their carefully written response. And it keeps going around."[5] When I first read this, it immediately resonated with me because Molly is describing something that happens over and over again in my church. Sometimes the correspondence is between just two people, but often these e-mails are sent with others copied or blind copied, causing the dispute to widen and escalate every time someone clicks "reply all."

It's just so tempting to conduct an argument by e-mail! Safely huddled behind our computer screens, we can carefully craft our arguments and score debate points in our own head, while never having to look the other person in the eye. We may feel better, at least until the next reply lands in our inbox. But this kind of exchange virtually never resolves the problem and usually makes it worse. In the tone-deaf environment of e-mail communication, subtleties and emotional shading go by the wayside. We are far more likely to misread the intent behind words or phrases and misjudge someone's motives. The result is a deepening divide rather than a meeting of the minds.

E-mail communication is an efficient way to handle many kinds of communication. But not when it comes to responding to complaints or criticism. I've taken to following Molly Phinney Baskette's advice: invite the person to sit down to discuss the issue face-to-face. When I receive a complaint by e-mail, I simply reply, "I don't think it's productive to deal with this issue by e-mail. Let's get together to talk." If there is something of substance to be discussed, you're far more likely to make progress in a real-time dialogue. If the other person really just wanted to sound off, they may well decline the invitation. But by refusing to take their bait, you've prevented the situation from escalating and avoided wasting time on an unproductive exchange, while at the same time opening the door to real communication.

MAKE THE EFFORT TO WORK WITH DIFFICULT PEOPLE

What about the finance chair who won't provide your team the budget information you need, the church matriarch who's always questioning your ideas, or the office administrator who's constantly putting roadblocks in front of your progress? Especially when working with a group, it's tempting to start talking this person down, even to the point of vilifying them. While it can be emotionally cathartic to complain about an obstreperous person, it doesn't advance the ball. In personalizing the dispute, you risk making an enemy of someone whose help and support you need. Taken to an extreme, this way of dealing with differences can lead to deeply entrenched factions.

When confronted with a particularly challenging person, I've taught myself to think of that person as "my new best friend." And I invest extra energy in working to bring the person around. It's far better to channel your energy into trying to work with a difficult person and stay on their good side than to let things devolve into an unproductive personality dispute.

KEEP YOUR EYE ON THE PRIZE

Someone once asked me what it was like to work for my church. "Well," I replied, "the really wonderful thing is that everything is a matter of principle. But the really difficult thing is that everything is a matter of principle." Church life is most motivating and rewarding when we engage at the level of our deepest passions. This is one factor that contributes to synergy. But passion can also give rise to intransigence, self-righteousness, and myopia, all of which can fuel conflict. In an emotionally charged environment, personality conflicts or disputes can absorb so much of our energy that they eclipse our ability to stay focused on the ministry to which God calls us. And systemic conflict can distract a whole congregation from its true mission.

If you find yourself in a situation where you think you need to be fighting a battle, scoring points, or ousting someone who doesn't see things the way you do, it's time for a reality check. During a major conflict in my church, I developed a simple, daily mantra. I told myself, "Keep your head down and do your job." Other members of the church take their cues from how those on staff and in leadership respond to a conflict. So make sure your actions communicate the importance of staying focused on the mission.

KEEP THINGS IN PERSPECTIVE

When we take on the leadership of a particular ministry, we often expect thanks and praise. After all, we're not doing it for our own sake but for the benefit of the church and to serve God. But the fact of the matter is whenever you take up the mantle of leadership, you become a lightning rod for criticism, whether it's deserved or not. It just goes with the territory. So it's important not to take things too personally. Again, this is easier said than done. But I've found that it does get easier with time and practice.

One of the benefits of cultivating some emotional objectivity in the face of criticism is that it allows us to learn from what's going on. Even if a complaint is truly unwarranted, it's helpful to consider what might have given rise to it. When we do our best to remain objective and take the perspectives of others seriously, conflicts and complaints can help us adapt to the realities of our ministry context and grow in positive ways. It's a type of feedback that can help us develop as synergistic leaders.

83

Discussion Questions

1. Many people seem to have a default setting when responding to conflict. Do you? If so, what is it? And what factors may have contributed to it?

2. Can you recall a time when you or someone else approached a conflict with enough emotional distance to think strategically about how best to respond?

3. How do you think leaders develop the maturity and discipline to avoid letting their emotions rule their responses to conflict?

4. Think back on a problem or conflict you've had to deal with. In retrospect, what might you have done differently?

PART THREE

_____

SPECIAL CONSIDERATIONS FOR CHURCH STAFF MEMBERS

CHAPTER TEN

Working Together for the Good of Those Who Love God

Leadership Perspectives for Church Employees

When first given the opportunity to work on the staff of my congregation, I couldn't have been more thrilled. I was excited to be able to devote myself full-time to the church I loved. I was intrigued to gain an insider's perspective on how it operated. I was motivated by the opportunity to be more significantly engaged in the congregation's mission. And, given that our culture values professionalism over volunteerism, I felt affirmed by having a title and a paycheck. Every other Friday, I'd find a paycheck in my cubby in the church mailroom, and I'd say to myself, "I can't believe I get paid for this!" Looking back, I have a fuller appreciation of how this opportunity was part of a call to a life of full-time Christian service that had unfolded over many years, beginning in childhood. But at the time, I was just happy to have a job doing what I loved. I had given very little thought to what it meant to be an employee of the church where I was also a member. Nor had I received any formal guidance on the matter.

For many, this is still a gray area, in part because the notion of a church staff that includes lay persons is a relatively recent phenomenon. In past generations, if a church had a staff, it was comprised of multiple clergy serving within the same congregation. Nonordained persons employed by the church were not considered members of the staff.[1] If a church needed to employ a secretary, custodian, or bookkeeper, they were often advised to hire someone from outside their congregation who would perform discrete tasks or functions. And these roles were seen as something apart from, or less than, the ministry of the clergy and the congregation.

But since the 1970s, as the number of lay persons working for churches has grown, there's also been a shift in the kind of jobs they perform. It's no longer the case that most lay staff members are in administrative or support roles. In my denomination, more than half of lay staff now work in a wide variety of programmatic ministries.[2] And congregations increasingly look to their own members to fill these roles. They want to hire someone who understands the spiritual DNA of the congregation and who has the relationships necessary to get things done. My research among lay staff in United Methodist churches found that 60 percent of survey respondents were members of the congregation they serve when they were hired. But at the time of the survey, 70 to 85 percent were members of the congregation where they worked, suggesting that lay hires who aren't church members when hired often join the church once on the job.[3]

This dual role, as congregant and church staff member, is one reason so many lay ministry professionals experience role ambiguity and tension. I often hear people say that the easiest way to avoid this dilemma is for congregations to have a rule against hiring their own members. Not only is this view out of step with current reality, it implies that someone is only capable of having one identity and role. Each of us constantly negotiates more than one set of roles and responsibilities. In my family, I am parent and child, wife and mother, sister, niece, aunt, cousin, and so on. In my workplace, I am supervisor to some, subordinate to others. Setting aside the question of employment, in most churches it's not only common but essential that people wear more than one hat. Someone might be a choir member, a Sunday school teacher, and a trustee. Is it sometimes confusing and messy? Yes. But it can also promote an interconnectedness that makes congregational life rich, rewarding, and dynamic. In this sense, it can be an element of synergy.

Anyone balancing different roles learns what's expected of each and how to behave accordingly. If we are employed by our church, we need to be clear about how our relationship to the church as employee differs from our relationship as a member. In their book on staffing and supervision in large congregations, *When Moses Meets Aaron*, Gil Rendle and Susan Beaumont draw a distinction between church members as *recipients* of ministry and church staff as *resources* for doing ministry.[4] Of course, it's not just paid staff who are in this dual role. Since all Christians are called to ministries of active service, to be a member of the body of Christ is to be both a recipient of ministry and an instrument of ministry. Nevertheless, Rendle and Beaumont's point is helpful. Church employees need to understand that in their paid role they are a resource for doing ministry and assume the attitude of Jesus when he said he "didn't come to be served but rather to serve" (Matt 20:28 CEB). We need to be quite clear about when and in what situations we are wearing the hat of a church staffer and when we are wearing the hat of a church member.

JOB DESCRIPTIONS

A clear job description is an invaluable tool in navigating this terrain. In chapter 5, I discussed how clearly defined roles reinforced through clear job descriptions contribute to synergistic teamwork. The same is true on a staff team. An accurate, detailed job description is your best guide to understanding how your job responsibilities differ from your activities as a church member.

Yet, for a variety of reasons, far too many church workers labor without the benefit of a formal job description—for example, the youth worker who was told only that he was to be the "education and youth guy."[5] As small employers, many congregations do not have well-developed human resource policies, and many pastors are not experienced in hiring and supervising staff. But more to the point, many churches hire staff without a clear vision for what the person will actually do, desperately hoping that adding staff will turn around a struggling area of ministry. This can be a surefire recipe for disaster. The staffer must labor with little guidance against sky-high expectations. Short of working a miracle, his or her efforts are likely to fall short. But at the same time, any initiative can run afoul of unspoken assumptions about what the job should entail. Vaguely defined job responsibilities can easily create a situation where you are damned if you do and damned if you don't.

It's ideal, of course, to have a job description in hand when you step into a staff role. But if you are already working without the benefit of a formal job description, you may need to take the initiative to get the ball rolling. Begin with your direct supervisor. Always frame the conversation in terms of your desire to enhance the church's ministry and do what is expected of you. Don't be surprised if there is indifference or even resistance toward the idea, especially if written job descriptions are something new within the church. It can be helpful to think of those critical junctures where it's logical to discuss your job responsibilities—in the context of a performance evaluation, for example, when there's transition on the staff team, or when a new pastor arrives. These are opportune moments to raise the question of a job description.

The exercise of drafting a job description for yourself can be a helpful exercise, even if no one else buys into the process. The first staff role I held in my church was director of stewardship. It was a new job, so there was no precedent regarding what duties it entailed. I was hired for my love of the church and my reputation for getting things done. But I knew precious little about Christian stewardship. The position had been created in part at the urging of an influential church member who had worked in university fundraising. He had very strong opinions about how things should be done. And our senior pastor, my boss, didn't always share the same perspective. So I was immediately triangulated between the two of them and two different visions of effective stewardship.

I quickly realized I needed to find my own way forward. I made learning everything I could about Christian stewardship my first priority. I read every book I could put my hands on. I visited with the staff of our denominational foundation and with the development officers of a nearby seminary. I looked for helpful learning events and attended whatever relevant workshops or seminars I could find. I even talked my way into stewardship trainings that our judicatory was providing to area clergy. Then, in consultation with some trusted colleagues and key leaders of the church, I started developing a set of goals to guide my work. I had essentially drafted my own job description, which I could then use as the basis of conversation with others to gain clarity around what was expected of me.

TRANSITIONS

If you are just beginning in a paid staff role, take stock of your other church involvements and consider which may need to be set aside in light of your new responsibilities. Consult your pastor, supervisor, or other church staff to see if there are precedents or policies in place. Is attending congregational meetings, events, and worship a part of your job responsibility, or something done on your own time? If you are also a member of the church, will you have voice and vote in church decision-making? Are you eligible to be nominated to lay leadership positions? Different congregations handle these matters in different ways. But gaining clarity around these questions can avoid confusion, conflict, and inconsistency.

Other issues come when a church member transitions out of a staff role. In many traditions, clergy are discouraged from participating in a congregation after they retire or transition into a different role. But many lay staff I know see their membership in the congregation as primary and choose to continue as a member, even if their employment ends. I know a dozen or more people in my church who have transitioned between paid and volunteer service, sometimes more than once. And for the most part, these changes have been graceful and grace-filled.

I transitioned off the staff of my church twice—once to concentrate on my seminary studies and the second time to go to work for a leadership center. Following each of these transitions, I stayed within the church but decided to focus on different activi-

Working Together for the Good of Those Who Love God

ties and involvements than the ones I had been responsible for as a paid staffer. For example, when I went to work for the leadership center, I decided to join a choir for the first time because it was something totally unrelated to my paid work. With the passage of time, I've gravitated back toward some areas of ministry where I previously worked, because they are where my greatest gifts and passions lie. But I remain on guard against the expectation that I can do in an unpaid role what I did as a full-time employee, whether it's an expectation I place on myself or one that others place on me. For me, the ability to stay connected to a single community of faith over many years is one of the greatest blessings of being a lay minister in a denomination where clergy itinerate. Remaining rooted in the same congregation has allowed me to reap the fruits of long-term relationships and see ministries flourish over many years, whether as a paid staffer or an unpaid ministry leader.

Perhaps the most challenging situation for someone who works for their church is if their job ends unhappily. Getting laid off or fired is painful and humiliating, and even more so when the drama is played out in front of your church family. The same is true if you are involved in a workplace dispute. This risk is something to be considered before accepting a job with your own church. And it underscores the importance of understanding that the relationship between employer and employee is a fundamentally different relationship than the covenant of church membership.[6] But the firing of a church member from a staff job certainly isn't the only difficult or awkward situation that can arise within a congregation. It has happened in my church. And while it wasn't easy for anyone involved, grace does abound.

SUPERVISION AND ACCOUNTABILITY

Because church staffers often function within complex, multilayered organizational systems, it's especially important to clarify lines of accountability. All ministry involves accountability to the broader faith community. And virtually every church leader must juggle multiple constituencies and competing priorities. But one of the greatest risks for a church employee comes when you are unsure about to whom you are directly accountable.

In some congregations, staff report to programmatic committees. "Especially if the staff person leads a program area like education, music, or youth work, which is 'owned' by a committee, it may seem natural," says Dan Hotchkiss, an expert on church leadership structures, "that the committee should hire, orient, and supervise that staff person."[7] But this arrangement is rife with potential confusion, triangulation, and conflict of interest. The staff member must satisfy a constantly changing group of bosses with different expectations and varying levels of knowledge about their work-a-day tasks and responsibilities. Moreover, in this arrangement, the staffer has no direct accountability to the church's overall mission or leadership, except through the committee. While it's logical for a program committee to have input into hiring or evaluating a staff member responsible for their area of ministry, an employee should be accountable to a single supervisor who can speak with one voice. In most churches, staff report to a senior pastor or another senior staff member who is present during working hours and therefore has direct knowledge of a staffer's activities.[8] A good job description should specify to whom you are directly accountable. If your reporting relationship is unspecified or confusing, you have a right to seek clarification.

The same is true with regard to employee evaluation systems. Periodic performance appraisal is standard in the workplace. But again, because many congregations have inadequate or flawed personnel policies, church staff sometimes work for extended periods of time without any formal evaluation or feedback. Or an evaluation is scheduled only when problems arise. Sometimes, anonymous input is solicited from the congregation in ways that risk making the evaluation process a popularity poll or a gripe session.[9] It behooves both congregations and their employees when well-thought-out review procedures are in place.

In the grand scheme of things, such questions about personnel policies might seem inconsequential or even self-interested. But right relationship is central to the gospel, and effective staff policies undergird the effectiveness of church workers and the congregations that employ them. Churches hire staff when aspects of their ministry require more leadership and attention than can reasonably be expected of a volunteer. So adequate and effective staffing is often a critical factor leading to vitality and growth. Sound employment policies give rise to synergistic ministry relationships.

CONFIDENTIALITY AND BOUNDARIES

When I was hired as stewardship director, I very quickly found myself privy to a great deal of information about fellow congregants, including people who were personal friends and acquaintances. Not only did I have access to their giving records, pastoral concerns related to sensitive health or family matters were often discussed around the staff table. Now, having worked in theological education for the past decade, I know how much training clergy receive on handling pastoral concerns, boundaries, and sexual ethics. And I cringe when I think back on how ill-prepared I was for this challenging aspect of ministry.

As more and more lay persons serve in ministry roles where they teach, lead, and counsel others, parishioners increasingly look to them for pastoral guidance and care. And lay staff who are members of the church where they work have some unique issues around confidentiality and boundaries because they are operating within long-standing relational networks and friendships. You protect yourself and others by complying with ethical boundaries and privacy standards. If no formal guidance is provided, seek advice from your pastor or other colleagues. If you work with children, in counseling, or in clinical settings, make it your business to know if there are any required safety or boundary trainings. Familiarize yourself with healthcare privacy standards. Be on guard when conversations turn to gossip. And make it a rule not to share information about someone else without their permission—even if you are doing it with the best of intentions.

MATTERS OF SPIRITUAL AUTHORITY

Because of my long-standing interest in the theology of lay ministry, when I conducted research among lay staff in United Methodist churches, I was particularly interested in their sense of theological identity. I discovered that many felt their ministry was encumbered by concerns related to their spiritual authority. Some reported that clergy and congregants failed to acknowledge their spiritual authority since they are not ordained. Others reported a lack of confidence about their spiritual ability, especially when congregants looked to them for spiritual leadership in areas where they felt unprepared or unsure of themselves.

Lay ministry practitioners often straddle the horns of a dilemma when it comes to matters of spiritual identity and standing. Sometimes, by virtue of our job responsibilities, we are expected to assume the attitudes, protocols, and responsibilities associated with ordained ministry. Other times, we bump up against the expectation in both church and culture that ministry is the purview of the ordained. And it can be quite tricky to figure out who expects you to behave in which manner and when. I often refer to this paradox as being perpetually "betwixt and between."

The chapters in the first part of this book are intended to assure lay ministry practitioners of the theological validity of our ministry and our callings. But gaining a sense of confidence in your spiritual leadership or being regarded as a spiritual authority within your ministry setting is more than a matter of theology. Spiritual authority and spiritual confidence do not come automatically by virtue of a job title. In any type of leadership, credibility is earned. We mature as spiritual leaders while we put our faith to work, demonstrating our love of God and others. And respect for our spiritual authority comes as people see us leading in spiritually sensitive ways. If we want others to regard our work as a ministry, then we need to bring the mind-set and practices of ministry to our work.

How might you enhance your spiritual confidence and authority? Think of the people whose spiritual leadership you admire. What gives credibility to their ministry? Find ways to grow in your knowledge of the Word and expand your theological understanding. Devote sufficient time to your own spiritual development and explore spiritual disciplines and practices that feed your soul. Become more conversant in the vocabulary of faith, and practice leading others in prayer, in public and private settings, until it feels comfortable. If you are in a behind-the-scenes role, discuss with others how you can make the spiritual dimensions of your ministry more evident to the congregation.

There may be people in your church who will always question the spiritual authority of a lay person with serious ministry responsibilities. And there will likely be people who continue to believe that churches should never hire their own members. But I have come to see the number of lay persons being called into significant ministry roles as an act of the Spirit to renew the church. It's an embodiment of the more inclusive, collaborative, synergistic approach to ministry that God is bringing forth in this day. We must hold fast to the belief that our spiritual empowerment and the legitimacy of our ministry comes from God, not from human authority.

Discussion Questions

1. What do you see as challenges for church staff who are also members of the church where they work?

2. Do staff in your church have clear, formal job descriptions? If not, how could they be created?

3. Do you think lay church employees have any unique challenges when it comes to issues related to confidentiality and boundaries in pastoral matters? What should be done?

4. What contributes to someone's spiritual authority? What can lay ministry practitioners do to enhance their sense of spiritual confidence and spiritual authority?

CHAPTER ELEVEN

Completing the Good Work Begun in You

Growing and Developing as a Leader

L
ike many people, I grew up with the admonition, "God helps those who help themselves." Much later, I learned this phrase isn't even in the Bible. And it even seems a bit contrary to New Testament norms. After all, shouldn't we concern ourselves more with serving others than advancing ourselves? And isn't mutuality more important than self-reliance? Yet it's also true that we become more effective as servants and instruments of collaborative ministry when we attend to our own need for spiritual formation, professional development, and leadership growth. When we take on a professional role, some of the responsibility for this growth falls on our own shoulders.

This self direction is especially true for lay persons in ministry because there are few structures in place to support our professional development and leadership growth. Those in ordained ministry are required to fulfill extensive educational requirements and undergo a period of candidacy, preparation, and examination. There are also agreed-upon structures for supervision, accountability, and support. For example, clergy often have continuing education requirements and are provided funds to fulfill those requirements. Because there are fewer standards and resources to assist lay ministry practitioners, we need to be more intentional and proactive in attending to these needs ourselves.

THINK OUTSIDE THE BOX

Clergy commonly develop professional relationships with other clergy in their community or their judicatory. But lay staff, particularly those who have been hired from within the congregation, often have few connections with faith communities other than their own local church. They end up siloed within their own congregation, trying to reinvent the wheel, in part because they aren't very familiar with how ministry is conducted in other settings.

You may be the only staff person responsible for children's ministry in your own congregation, but there could be like-minded leaders with similar responsibilities and challenges in other nearby churches, whether they are part of your same denomination or not. Check out the websites of other churches in your community or region. Do they seem to have a strong program in your area of ministry? Is there a staff member responsible? If so, get on the phone, introduce yourself, and ask some questions about their ministry model. If it sounds like the person you're speaking with is knowledgeable and accessible, suggest getting together for lunch or coffee. Or ask if you can visit the church to learn more about their programming. If the relationship proves productive, you might consider getting together regularly. Forging ties with peers working in other churches is a great way to share ideas, resources, and best practices. A peer support network can also be an external sounding board and a source of support and camaraderie.

In some areas of specialization, such as church administration, sacred music, and Christian education, professional associations and guilds can provide this type of enrichment and support.

Workshops, seminars, and other training events are another important means of professional development. Subscribing to on-line newsletters and blogs will give you a sense of what's offered in your field. Ask your pastor or supervisor for help in identifying appropriate learning resources and if there are funds available to cover the cost. Many denominations and seminaries offer certification programs for ministry professionals in areas such as youth ministry, church administration, Christian education, music, and health ministry. And with more and more classes being offered online, you may be able to advance your theological education without interrupting your career.

FIND MENTORS

In virtually every field of endeavor, there is mounting evidence to suggest that having the right mentors is a critical factor in achieving success. Research on effectiveness in ministry bears this out. And so does the Bible. In Scripture, mentoring is the principal instrument used by God to shape individuals as leaders. The relationships between Moses and Joshua, Naomi and Ruth, Eli and Samuel, Elijah and Elisha, Elizabeth and Mary, Barnabas and Paul, and Jesus and his disciples are just a few examples of how God used mentors to prepare leaders in biblical times.

Sometimes, one has the benefit of a formal mentor—someone who is assigned or signs on to the task of assisting in another's development, usually for an extended period of time. But more often, mentoring happens in less formal ways, through many different relationships. Effective leaders learn to search out a diverse group of people who are willing to share their expertise and wisdom. If you need to master a new competency, if you're thinking through a knotty problem, or if you need the story behind a long-simmering dispute, ask, "Who are the wise people I could consult?" It may be someone from within your congregation, perhaps someone with specialized professional skills. Or it may be someone from a totally different walk of life. Generally, people are flattered when you ask for their advice or help. It requires a certain humility to acknowledge that you don't know all the answers. But making a practice of engaging others in support of your ministry goals is synergistic collaboration at its best.

FEED YOUR SOUL

A common challenge among church workers, whether clergy or lay, is that their job responsibilities can prevent them from drawing spiritual sustenance from the worship and community life within the congregation they serve. If you're leading children's activities or responsible for hospitality, you may never darken the door of the sanctuary on Sunday mornings. If you're running the soundboard, the finer points of the sermon may be lost on you. If you're in the chancel directing the choir, you may long for the opportunity to worship in the pew alongside your spouse or family members. And if you're in charge of facilities, you're probably praying with one eye open, knowing that news of an overflowing toilet could come at any time. Similarly, if you've moved from the congregation into a staff role, participating in the same groups and classes may no longer feel right. Whatever the reason, if your spiritual thirst is no longer quenched by the normal activities of your church, you need to drink from a different well.

Congregations with larger staffs will often integrate prayer, Bible study, spiritual formation, and even regular worship into the ongoing work of their staff team. And the pastor or another experienced staff member may take the lead in mentoring the spiritual development of other team members. Some staffs function as a covenant group, with clear expectations around mutual accountability, communication, and spiritual growth.[1]

But other ministry professionals find that they need to look beyond the congregation for spiritual sustenance. I know church workers who attend evening services in other faith communities so that they can worship without the distraction of feeling responsible for what's going on. Others seek out retreats, pilgrimages, or learning events sponsored by other religious organizations. It's also important to redouble your commitment to personal spiritual disciplines, such as prayer, Scripture reading, fasting, journaling, or meditation. Tending your own soul will not only add credibility to your spiritual leadership, it will also be a powerful example to other laity in your congregation. For this reason, personal growth and development are vital, yet often overlooked, factors in synergy. When we take our own leadership and spiritual growth seriously, we become models for others in the church, particularly other laity.

THE SYNERGY OF GOD'S FUTURE

Paul and Silas in Thessalonica, after preaching in the synagogue, were joined by a great many devout Greeks and not a few of the leading women of that community. The Jews became jealous and complained to the city authorities that these apostles of the early church were turning the world upside down (Acts 17:6). Throughout all of salvation history, God is turning the world upside down—turning it upside down in order to set it straight—whether delivering a band of runaway slaves to the Promised Land, calling a shepherd boy to be king, or sending a Messiah born in a stable.

While my passion for the ministry of the laity is born in part of my own experience, it also springs from a deep theological conviction that the leadership necessary to revitalize the church in these challenging times is more likely to come from the bottom up than from the top down. It's difficult for me to draw any other conclusion from the witness of Scripture. I see powerful evidence of this reversal in the way God is raising up so many new and different leaders in this era when the church is struggling against institutional decline.

While my focus in this book is on lay ministry professionals, God's desire to expand ministry is certainly not limited to those who serve the church through paid employment. Theologically, ministry is never defined by professionalism, position, or paycheck. But those of us who have the privilege of working for the church can devote considerably more time to Christian service than those who earn their living in others ways. And our ministries are often more visible. So we can model for others what it means to be spiritually empowered and radically committed Christian servants. When we allow God to use us in this way, we help others understand the true nature of ministry and the inclusivity of God's call. This is, I believe, the spiritual synergy that God will use to lead the body of Christ forward. Your commitment, your ministry, and your leadership matter in ways beyond just the immediate focus of your work. They are embodiments of the synergistic approach to ministry that God intended from the start. Let us be so!

Notes

INTRODUCTION

1. Ann Albrecht Michel, "The New Church Leaders: Lay Ministry Professionals in the United Methodist Church" (Doctor of Ministry Project Thesis, Wesley Theological Seminary, 2011).

2. Zeni Fox, *Lay Ecclesial Ministry: Pathways toward the Future* (Landham, MD: Rowman and Littlefield, 2010), 198.

1. WORKING TOGETHER

1. Dwight Zscheile, "Leadership Multiplication and the Way of Jesus," *Leading Ideas* Electronic Newsletter, June 7, 2006, www.churchleadership.com/leading-ideas/leadership-multiplication-and-the-way-of-jesus/.

2. George Barna, *The Power of Team Leadership* (Colorado Springs: WaterBrook Press), 22.

3. Efrain Agosto, *Servant Leadership: Jesus and Paul* (St. Louis: Chalice Press, 2005), 121.

4. Agosto, *Servant Leadership: Jesus and Paul*, 121.

5. Douglas Stewart, *World Biblical Commentary Vol. 31, Hosea–Jonah* (Waco, TX: World Books Publisher, 1987), 230.

6. Thomas P. Rausch, "Ministry and Ministries," in *Ordering the Baptismal Priesthood*, ed. Susan K .Woods (Collegeville, MN: Liturgical Press, 2003), 54.

2. WHO, ME? YES, YOU!

1. Os Guinness, *The Call* (Nashville: World Publishing, 2003), 30–31.
2. William C. Placher, ed., *Callings: Twenty Centuries of Christian Wisdom on Vocation* (Grand Rapids: Eerdmans, 2005), 206.
3. Guinness, *The Call*, 27–29.
4. Zeni Fox and Regina Bechtle, eds., *Called and Chosen: Toward a Spirituality for Lay Leaders* (Lanham, MD: Rowman and Littlefield, 2005), 4.

3. AT YOUR SERVICE

1. Thomas F. O'Meara, *Theology of Ministry,* rev. ed. (New York: Paulist Press, 1999), 95.
2. Gary D. Badcock, *The Way of Life* (Grand Rapids: Eerdmans, 1998), 97.
3. Kenan Osborne, *Orders and Ministry* (Maryknoll, NY: Orbis Books, 2006), 42.
4. Rausch, "Ministry and Ministries," 53.
5. Ibid., 52–53.
6. Osborne, *Orders and Ministry,* 42.
7. Edward P. Hahnenberg, *Ministries: A Relational Approach* (New York: Crossroads, 2003), 24.
8. Michael Downey, "Ministerial Identity: A Question of Common Foundations," in *Ordering the Baptismal Priesthood,* ed. Susan K. Woods (Collegeville, MN: Liturgical Press, 2003), 5–6.
9. Dennis M. Campbell, *The Yoke of Obedience: The Meaning of Ordination in Methodism* (Nashville: Abingdon, 1988), 21.
10. Patricia N. Page, *All God's People Are Ministers* (Minneapolis: Augsburg Press, 1993), 28.

4. THE HEART OF THE MATTER

1. Hahnenberg, *Ministries: A Relational Approach,* 5.
2. Lovett H. Weems, Jr., "Relationships Are Everything," *Lead-*

ing Ideas Electronic Newsletter, December 7, 2011, https://www
.churchleadership.com/leading-ideas/relationships-are-everything/.

3. Matt Haber, "They Want to Be Like Mark," *New York Times,*
February 28, 2016.

5. BODY BUILDING

1. Barna, *The Power of Team Leadership,* 29.

2. Ibid., 81.

3. Ibid., 23.

4. Ibid., 24.

5. Ibid., 123.

6. Patrick Lencioni, *Overcoming the Five Dysfunctions of a Team,*
Kindle edition (San Francisco: Jossey-Bass, 2005), location 67.

7. James M. Kouzes and Barry Z. Posner, *The Leadership Challenge,* 3rd ed. (San Francisco: Jossey-Bass, 2002), 253.

8. Barna, *The Power of Team Leadership,* 25.

9. Dan Hotchkiss, *Governance and Ministry,* 1st ed. (Herndon,
VA: Alban Institute, 2009), 67.

10. Lencioni, *Overcoming the Five Dysfunctions of a Team,* location 56–61.

11. Ibid., location 133.

6. FOLLOW ME

1. Charles R. Lane, *Ask, Thank, Tell: Improving Stewardship Ministry in Your Congregation* (Minneapolis: Augsburg Fortress, 2006), 95.

7. TWO BY TWO

1. Zscheile, "Leadership Multiplication and the Way of Jesus."

2. Tony Morgan, "3 Sure-Fire Ways to Fail in Developing Leaders," *Leading Ideas* Electronic Newsletter, May 11, 2016, www
.churchleadership.com/leading-ideas/3-surefire-ways-to-fail-in
-developing-leaders/.

3. Stewart Perry, "Coaching New Leaders," *Leading Ideas* Electronic Newsletter, February 15, 2006, https://www.churchleadership.com/leading-ideas/coaching-new-leaders-3/.

4. I learned about this progression of leadership development in the Gospels from Tim Keel, pastor of Jacob's Well in Kansas City, Missouri, during a presentation he made to a Lewis Center leadership development cohort.

5. Some translations of the Bible report the number of people that Jesus sent out as seventy-two rather than seventy.

6. John W. Wimberly, Jr., *Mobilizing Congregations: How Teams Can Motivate Members and Get Things Done* (Lanham, MD: Rowman and Littlefield, 2015), 1–3.

7. Reggie McNeal, *A Work of Heart: Understanding How God Shapes Spiritual Leaders* (San Francisco: Jossey-Bass, 2000), 61.

8. WHERE TWO OR MORE ARE GATHERED

1. Stephen R. Covey, *The 7 Habits of Highly Effective People* (New York: Fireside Books, 1989), 97.

2. Lovett H. Weems, Jr., and Tom Berlin, *Bearing Fruit: Ministry with Real Results* (Nashville: Abingdon, 2011), 20.

3. Lencioni, *Overcoming the Five Dysfunctions of a Team,* location 377.

4. Hotchkiss, *Governance and Ministry,* 148.

5. Lencioni, *Overcoming the Five Dysfunctions of a Team,* location 476.

6. Ibid., location 434.

9. QUICK TO HEAR, SLOW TO SPEAK AND ANGER

1. Lovett H. Weems, Jr., "Promise and Peril: Understanding and Managing Change and Conflict in Congregations," *Leading Ideas* Electronic Newsletter, August 4, 2010, https://www.churchleadership.com/leading-ideas/promise-and-peril-understanding-and-managing-change-and-conflict-in-congregations/.

2. Norma Cook Everist, *Church Conflict: From Contention to Collaboration* (Nashville: Abingdon, 2004).

3. Ronald Richardson, *Creating a Healthier Church: Family Systems Theory, Leadership, and Congregational Life* (Minneapolis: Fortress Press, 1996), 114.

4. Ibid., 114.

5. Molly Phinney Baskette, *Real Good Church* (Cleveland: Pilgrim Press, 2014), 57.

10. WORKING TOGETHER FOR THE GOOD OF THOSE WHO LOVE GOD

1. Kenneth Mitchell, *Multiple Staff Ministries* (Philadelphia: Westminster Press, 1988), 22.

2. Michel, "The New Church Leaders," 15–16.

3. Ibid., 36.

4. Gil Rendle and Susan Beaumont, *When Moses Meets Aaron: Staffing and Supervision in Large Congregations* (Herndon, VA: Alban Institute, 2007), 10–11.

5. Alan Rudnick, *The Work of the Associate Pastor* (Valley Forge, PA: Judson Press), 34.

6. Rendle and Beaumont, *When Moses Meets Aaron,* 23.

7. Dan Hotchkiss, *Governance and Ministry,* 51–52.

8. Ibid., 51–52.

9. Ibid., 143–44.

11. COMPLETING THE GOOD WORK BEGUN IN YOU

1. George Cladis, *Leading the Team-Based Church* (San Francisco: Jossey-Bass, 1999), 33.

CPSIA information can be obtained
at www.ICGtesting.com
Printed in the USA
LVOW03s2304140417
530933LV00006B/17/P